LEAVESDEN
AERODROME

FROM HALIFAXES
TO HOGWARTS

LEAVESDEN AERODROME

FROM HALIFAXES
TO HOGWARTS

GRANT PEERLESS & RICHARD RIDING

AMBERLEY

For Ian Honeywood, who sadly passed away in December 2009. He had been researching the history of Leavesden Aerodrome and associated aircraft factories for over fifteen years with a view to writing a book. When we discovered this, we got together and discussed a joint venture but understandably Ian had decided to fulfill his ambition and publish a book in his own name. Unfortunately, he was not able to complete the project. He was, however, a great help to us in preparing this book and was extremely generous in letting us use his material and photographs, which he had painstakingly assembled. We hope that this book goes some way to realising Ian's dream. It has certainly been enriched by his valuable contribution.

And for E. J. 'Eddie' Riding (1916–50), whose involvement with Leavesden Aerodrome sparked the original idea for this book.

First published 2011

Amberley Publishing
The Hill, Stroud
Gloucestershire GL5 4EP

www.amberleybooks.com

Copyright © Grant Peerless and Richard Riding 2011

The right of Grant Peerless and Richard Riding to be identified as the Authors of this work has been asserted in accordance with the Copyrights, Designs and Patents Act 1988.

British Library Cataloguing in Publication Data.
A catalogue record for this book is available from the British Library.

ISBN 978-1-4456-0418-3

Typeset in 10pt on 12pt Sabon.
Typesetting and Origination by Amberley Publishing.
Printed in the UK.

CONTENTS

INTRODUCTIONS

I first visited Leavesden Aerodrome in the mid-1950s, probably during one of de Havilland's regular open days. These popular events provided a rare opportunity to have a good look at the delights to be discovered inside the big green hangar down the hill on the far side of the airfield. At other times avid spotters like myself had to climb up the embankment from the A41 and peer through the fence. On one occasion, the de Havilland open day coincided with a flying display at nearby Elstree Aerodrome, and this involved a frantic cycle ride along the Watford bypass in order to catch both events.

I continued calling at Leavesden over the years, my last visit being just before it closed. I now see the former aerodrome from a different perspective as I fly regularly from Elstree Aerodrome with a pilot friend. A north-westerly departure usually takes us over the site, which is now occupied by Leavesden Studios. At the time of writing, some of the wartime buildings survive but with extensive developments taking place at the studios their days may be numbered.

It is sad to note that in the 1950s and 1960s aircraft enthusiasts had the choice of six airfields in Hertfordshire: Bovingdon, Radlett, Hatfield, Leavesden, Elstree and Panshanger. Now, sadly, only the latter two survive.

Grant Peerless
St Albans
March 2011

From 1942 until 1946 my father, E. J. Riding, was an Aeronautical Inspection Department (AID) inspector assigned first to London Aircraft Production (LAP) and later to the de Havilland Aircraft Company at Leavesden Aerodrome. He signed out Handley Page Halifaxes at LAP until June 1944, when he was transferred to the other side of the aerodrome. The same sort of work continued on various marks of Mosquito until he left there in February 1946.

On several occasions in 1945–46 I was taken to Leavesden and although only aged four I well remember the exciting harmonic strains of Rolls-Royce Merlin engines being run up prior to flight testing; it is a sound that evokes a deep sense of nostalgia even to this day.

It would be a further twenty-two years before I visited Leavesden again, landing as a passenger in a Cessna 'push-pull' 337 Skymaster. We parked outside the green Mosquito flight shed, but its doors were firmly closed and it would be another few years before I was able to look inside, during visits to see Mike Searle. In 1970 I did some local flying with Don Kendall in an Alon A-2 Aircoupe and during the following year had several flights in the first imported AA-1 Yankees that were assembled at Leavesden for a period.

My two most exciting flights from Leavesden were made in the American Goodyear airship N2A in June 1973, cruising sedately around the local countryside at 35 knots at 1,500 feet. I recall that in order to land, the pilot, Arnaud Brizon, pointed the nose of the airship down at an angle of what appeared to be 45 degrees and aimed the airship at the gathering ground crew below. At the last moment, Arnaud wound back the big wheel by his side and the ship bottomed out as many pairs of hands grabbed the dangling mooring ropes and hung on to them while we stepped out, the ground handlers occupying the gondola as we did so.

A few months later I did some flying in a Bell 206B Jet Ranger, flown by a former US military chopper pilot. Apparently, a few days later, the pilot climbed out of the same aircraft somewhat spooked, vowing never to fly a chopper again.

From then on I made only occasional visits to Leavesden. Then, one day in 1994, it was gone – or at least it was closed to flying. If you drive off the slip road at Junction 19 on the M25 heading east today, ahead on the rising ground, partly hidden by trees, can still be seen the green Mosquito flight sheds. Every time I see them my mind slips back to those immediate post-war days when, holding on to my Dad's hand, I'd watch, slightly fearful, as another pair of Merlin engines bellowed out their magical, unforgettable harmony. What memories.

Richard Riding
Radlett
March 2011

CHAPTER ONE

THE BEGINNING

The Question of an Aerodrome for Watford

The need for a municipal aerodrome for the Hertfordshire town of Watford was debated at length by the town council for nearly eight years. Eventually, in 1940, the Air Ministry decided the issue by requisitioning land at Leavesden for an aircraft factory and airfield.

Our story, however, begins in 1929, when Sir Alan Cobham, an avid supporter of British aviation and organiser of National Aviation Days, toured over a hundred towns and cities in the United Kingdom by air to impress upon senior council officials the need for them to provide local aerodromes. Sadly Watford was not included on his itinerary. Then, in February 1932, the Watford Light Aero Club (a.k.a. Watford Artisans Flying Club) had nearly completed work on Sopwith Scooter aircraft G-EACZ and was looking for a suitable field from which to fly it. The club therefore turned to the town council for help and suggested two possible sites: the field adjoining the isolation hospital, which was owned by the council, and a site near Hunters Lane at Leavesden known locally as One Mile Field, which was owned by Mr E. H. Loyd of Langleybury. The town council debated the request and appointed a sub-committee to consider and report on the matter.

Sir Alan Cobham Intervenes

The Light Aero Club also enlisted the support of Sir Alan Cobham, who considered that one of the best ways to draw the site to the council's attention would be to bring his National Aviation Day display to the town. This never happened; the nearest displays took place at Kings Langley and Aldenham in April 1933. In order to further the aerodrome suggestion, Lady Cobham surveyed the site at Leavesden and immediately saw that the field was ideal for an aerodrome. 'It will be a crying shame if the field is not turned into one,' she said.

An Early Film Studio Proposal

With a foretaste of things to come, One Mile Field was also being considered for film studios and the Abbots Langley Parochial Committee preferred this idea to a new aerodrome. Unsurprisingly, the film company concerned also objected to the aerodrome proposal.

The Debate Continues

The sub-committee appointed to consider the provision of a municipal aerodrome duly made its report to the town council in late July 1932 and unfortunately recommended that no proceedings be taken in the matter, but reserved the right to reconsider it should the film company fail to commence operations within six months. The sub-committee further stated that the borough surveyor had had an interview with the Civil Aviation Department of the Air Ministry and had been informed that there were no grants whatsoever available to municipal authorities, either for the purchase of land or the construction of an aerodrome. A rough estimate of the cost of an aerodrome at the Leavesden Green site was said to be £59,400 (about £3 million today). After this flurry of activity, no more was heard about the proposal for an aerodrome or film studios for nearly two years until, in March 1934, the question of a municipal airport was raised again. The mayor and council officers met with the Air Ministry and Ministry of Health with the result that the Finance Committee decided to appoint an aviation consultant. Accordingly, Mr Nigel Norman of Heston was appointed for a fee of £65 (about £3,300 today) to make a survey of the neighbourhood to find a suitable site. He identified such a site, but its location was not divulged to the public. The Air Ministry considered his report and, subject to their requirements being fulfilled, they were prepared to issue a licence enabling the site to be used as an aerodrome for all types of aircraft and for flying instruction. The district valuer was then requested to provide a valuation of the proposed site.

Flying Fair

In the meantime a 'Flying Fair' organised by Aviation Developments Ltd (proprietor Ronald Dixey-Gerrans) was held at Hunters Farm, Leavesden, on 8–9 April 1934 and included an air display, parachute jumps, joy rides etc. It claimed to be the first of its kind to tour Great Britain, but Sir Alan Cobham and other outfits had been running similar events since 1919. It is interesting that the site chosen was close to (or possibly the same as) the future Leavesden Aerodrome.

A Fire Bell Sounds Defeat

In October 1934, the Finance Committee received a preliminary report and estimate for a municipal aerodrome, including particulars from four other towns that had established aerodromes. Accordingly Mr Norman was requested to advise on companies that might be interested in operating an aerodrome. A subsequent editorial in the *West Herts Post* suggested that any proposal for an airport should be considered from the point of view of both commercial enterprise and national defence and should be subsidised by the Air Ministry. The Abbots Langley Parochial Committee then considered a report from a town planning consultant, Mr W. R. Davidge, which suggested a location for the proposed aerodrome.

He stated that in view of the town council's proposed acquisition of a large area of land on the south side of Hunters Lane, Leavesden, for an aerodrome, it would be advisable to keep approaches free from buildings so as not to interfere with

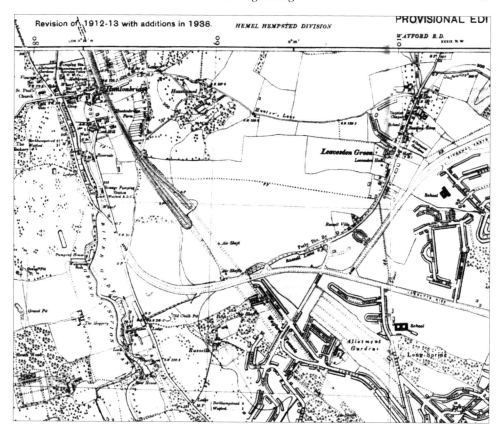

1938 Ordnance Survey 6 inch–1 mile map showing the site of the proposed Leavesden aerodrome on Mile Field – so named because of its approximate dimensions. (*Reproduced from the Ordnance Survey map with the kind permission of the Ordnance Survey*)

flying. This site was confirmed at the town council meeting on 1 January 1935, and it was described thus: 'on one side is the Leavesden High Road, on the other is the By-Pass Road and quite close is the North Orbital Road'. This was the site recommended by Mr Norman and belonged to E. Henry Loyd of Langleybury. It comprised 118.5 acres and the asking price was £25,000 (about £1.32 million today). Also announced at the meeting was an offer from a company prepared to establish a flying school on the site and from another to provide workshops and operate an airport. Unfortunately the council deferred making a decision and asked for a further 'exhaustive' report to be submitted. This was duly presented to a meeting a month later; the voting was fourteen for and fourteen against the proposal to acquire the land. In a quirk of fate, a councillor who would have supported the aerodrome proposal was called away. The councillor in question happened to be the chairman of the Fire Brigade Committee – he had heard a fire engine bell and left the meeting to find out where the fire was. The motion was therefore defeated by the chairman's casting vote. When he eventually returned to the council chamber it was too late to vote. One councillor in particular was not happy with the outcome. Asked at a subsequent meeting of the National

League of Airmen if Watford could have an aerodrome, she replied that she had negotiated with Mr Loyd for three years and that the outcome was perfectly scandalous. In May 1935 the council re-affirmed its decision not to proceed with the aerodrome proposal and agreed instead to purchase the same land for playing field purposes.

The County Council Intervenes

The idea of an aerodrome was not dead, however, because in July 1935 all town planning authorities in Hertfordshire were asked by the county council to 'give consideration to the desirability of reserving or acquiring, as may be appropriate, such sites as may be considered necessary for the purposes of aerodromes'. It went on to say, 'With the spread of aerial transport, the provision of suitable aerodromes is likely, in the near future, to become a question of great importance and places which do not possess the necessary facilities will be under a considerable handicap.' The county council suggested that local authorities consult the Aerodrome Advisory Board of the Air Ministry for advice on the selection and layout of sites for aerodromes. This advice was duly considered by the town council, who were informed by the Air Ministry that the amount of equipment necessary at a municipal aerodrome would depend on the volume of its traffic and that the ministry would have an idea of the volume when a survey of future internal airlines had been completed. Not surprisingly, the council decided to defer further consideration pending the receipt of additional details from the Air Ministry.

The Public's Views Are Requested

However, the question of an aerodrome would not go away and an article in the *West Herts Post* in August 1935 asked if Watford was right or wrong in rejecting the proposal, particularly as a network of airways linking up Great Britain had been planned. Imperial Airways, in conjunction with Railway Air Services, was planning a network radiating from a new base on the south coast, which would be the terminus of both the empire services and a proposed trans-Atlantic route. The article went on to say that twenty-three municipalities already had their own airports, five more had acquired sites, and four had reserved sites. It questioned whether Watford was too near London to reap any benefit from joining them – or would the capital welcome a Croydon on its northern side? The newspaper followed this article by asking its readers to say in as few words as possible why they thought Watford should or should not have a municipal aerodrome. All those replying were offered free admission to the forthcoming finals of the King's Cup Air Race to be held at Hatfield. Interestingly, voting was two to one in favour of the idea, but nothing was to come of it. Then, in June 1936, the council decided to ask Hertfordshire County Council if it thought favourable consideration would be given to the establishment of a municipal aerodrome at a different site, this time on the Red Heath Estate, Croxley Green, an area of 400–500 acres thought to be ideal for an aerodrome. It was pointed out that Luton, the town's near neighbour, had an airport so why couldn't Watford? Not surprisingly, nothing came of this suggestion.

Aerodrome Proposal Defeated Again

The aerodrome question was again debated at length by the town council in July 1936 and concentrated on the principle, not the site. But it was still undecided; not surprisingly the matter was adjourned until the following September. Following this meeting, the *West Herts Post* again invited readers to give their opinion on the matter and offered a prize of half a guinea (£25 today) for the best letter. This time public opinion was against the proposal, mainly on the grounds of cost, and also it was felt that any expenditure should be borne by the Government. Needless to say, when the matter was discussed again in September, the council did not come to a final decision but referred it to the Town Planning Committee for further discussion. The matter was not considered again until January 1937, when the town clerk reported to the Town Planning Committee that he had had discussions with a company interested in the running of aerodromes. The committee agreed to set up yet another sub-committee to consider the proposals, consult the county council and the Air Ministry, and report back. This came to nothing, however, and in June that year the council recommended no alteration to the use of the King George V Recreation Ground (as the site originally earmarked for an aerodrome at Leavesden was now called) and was not prepared to entertain any suggestion for the use of the land as an aerodrome.

An Alternative Proposal is Put Forward

However, this was not the last word. A month later Watford Town Council turned its attention instead to the aerodrome at Aldenham (Elstree) and considered developing it as its municipal aerodrome. The Air Ministry was consulted on the proposal and was of the opinion that it could be done but would require a good deal of levelling, filling and the diversion or placing underground of nearby high-tension electricity cables. The site was also outside the borough, some 4 miles from the town, and had poor access by rail. Although the planned extension of the Northern Line to Bushey Heath would have provided a new station near the site, this was abandoned with the outbreak of the Second World War and was never revived. The town council was unhappy that the Air Ministry was not prepared to make any financial contribution towards the cost of improvements, conservatively estimated to be £100,000 (about £5 million today), and the proposal did not proceed. This effectively signaled the end of any further attempts to secure an aerodrome for Watford.

The King George V Recreation Ground

Ambitious plans for transforming the King George V Recreation Ground, the seventh of Watford's recreation grounds, were put before the town council in July 1937. The estimated cost was £30,000 (about £1.44 million today) and the necessary land, part of Hunters Farm, was purchased from Mr E. H. Loyd of Langleybury. It is not clear how much work, if any, was carried out before war was declared, but interestingly, 'King George V Recreation Ground' is marked on the 1939 1:2500 Ordnance Survey Map; no other features appear.

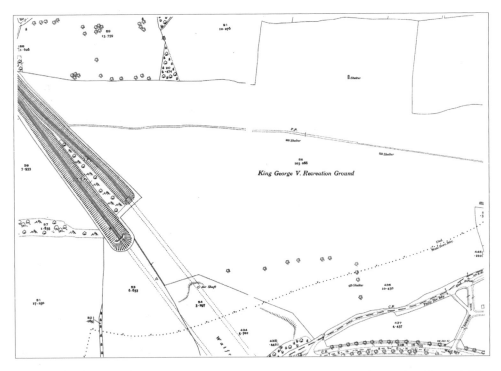

A 1939 Ordnance Survey 1:2500 map clearly shows King George V Recreation Ground. Not reproduced to scale. (*Reproduced from the Ordnance Survey map with the kind permission of the Ordnance Survey*)

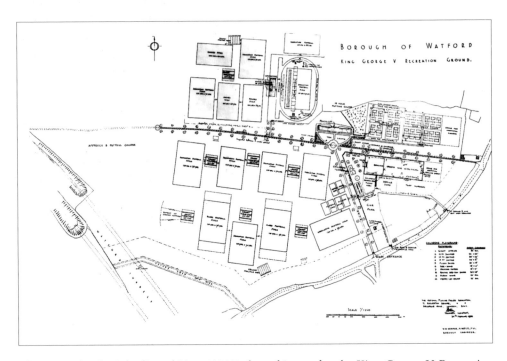

The Borough of Watford's ambitious 1937 plan of intent for the King George V Recreation Ground, prepared by W. Newman, borough engineer. The drawing was endorsed by the National Playing Field Association on 24 February 1938. (*Craig Woods*)

CHAPTER TWO

THE SECOND WORL

Leavesden Aerodrome Is Born

Following the outbreak of the Second World War the Handley Page Aircraft Company suggested that, in order to accelerate construction of its Halifax four-engined bomber, a sub-contracting scheme should be set up in the London area under the control of the de Havilland Company (DH). At around the same time, DH had been approached to build Armstrong Whitworth Albermarles (later the order switched to Vickers Wellington bombers). DH was happy to assist in setting up a production facility for the Halifax but was of the opinion that any sub-contracting should rest with Handley Page. DH set about finding a location for a shadow factory/aerodrome and flew surveys to identify a suitable site. They soon settled on the King George V Recreation Ground to the west of Leavesden village, also known as 'Mile Field' because of its approximate dimensions. As the Cobhams had earlier concluded, this was the obvious choice for an aerodrome as it was a flat area of non-agricultural land adjacent to a centre of population offering employment potential, as well as having excellent road communications.

Accordingly, on 10 January 1940, DH was requested by the Air Ministry to go ahead with the preparation of an aerodrome on the site, together with factories for aircraft assembly. DH's involvement in the Leavesden project was confirmed in a letter from the Ministry of Aircraft Production (MAP) dated 22 January 1940. (The MAP was set up in 1940 to be responsible for aircraft production and was abolished in 1946, its duties reverting to the Ministry of Supply. This in turn was abolished in 1959 and responsibilities devolved to three single-service units, which were later merged to form the Ministry of Defence in 1964.) The Air Ministry then acquired the land from Watford Borough Council for £5,000 (about £203,000 today) by compulsory purchase on behalf of the MAP, but the 300 acres actually purchased was considerably more than the 118 acres originally bought for playing field use. George Wimpey Ltd commenced construction straight away on a 3,033-foot concrete runway 150 feet wide aligned roughly north-east–south-west, together with two separate factory areas, one adjacent to Leavesden Village (No. 2 Factory) and the other half a mile to the west, to the north of the runway towards Kings Langley (No. 1 Factory). Both factory units were connected to the runway by taxiways and ground running sheds were provided adjacent to the factory areas. Two flight clearance/rectification sheds were also constructed – one adjacent to the normal take-off end and the other one at the western end of the runway, conveniently placed for the reception of aircraft after flight testing. In

the factories and airfield were reported to be taking shape. During
nsideration was given to extending and realigning the runway so as
de increased safety for aircraft operations, but this idea was eventually
ped when major aircraft production was scaled down.

A pre-war view of Mile Field shortly before it was absorbed into Leavesden aerodrome. The last hay crop is about to be gathered in. (*Rolls-Royce*)

The rear of Hunters Hall, leading to what was to become the main gate. (*Rolls-Royce*)

This is believed to be the first phase in the construction of Leavesden aerodrome, near the main gate and orchard. (*BAE Systems*)

Construction is underway in early 1940. This is probably No. 1 Factory looking towards Hunton Lodge and the entrance. (*BAE Systems*)

The No. 2 Factory canteen building taking shape in early 1941; the Hunters Hall chimney pots can be seen on the left. (*BAE Systems*)

Nearing completion in 1941 is the standalone hangar at No. 2 Factory. This became the turbine blades shop in the 1970s. (*BAE Systems*)

The runway end of the No. 2 Factory in 1941, before the extension was added. (*BAE Systems*)

The No. 2 Factory and boiler house, near the main gate, in 1941. (*BAE Systems*)

The completed camouflaged Mosquito Flight Shed No. 1 in 1948 with a lone Mosquito bottom right. The A41 road can be seen top right. (*BAE Systems*)

This 1948 aerial view shows the No. 1 Factory and the temporary white control tower, raised to offer a view over the yet-to-be-built main office block. (*BAE Systems*)

This view of No. 2 Factory, de Havilland Aircraft Company, shows a couple of Mosquitoes outside. South Way runs diagonally across the photograph. Hill Farm can be seen bottom right. (*BAE Systems*)

A similar view to the above but also showing No. 1 Factory at the top of the photograph. Hunters Lane can be seen at the left-hand edge.

Halifax Production

On 12 March 1940, the MAP issued an order to DH for 150 Halifax bombers but this was quickly terminated on 20 May and replaced with one for the construction of Armstrong Whitworth Albemarles, twin-engined light bombers, later changed to Vickers Wellingtons. With DH now out of the picture discussions began in earnest to achieve the production of the Halifaxes. The London Aircraft Production Group (LAPG) was subsequently formed, which comprised local firms involved in the motor industry. They were London Passenger Transport Board (LPTB) of Chiswick & Aldenham, Express Motors & Body Works of Enfield, Chrysler Motors of Kew, Duple Bodies & Motors of Hendon, and Park Royal Coachworks of Neasden. The LPTB was responsible for the co-ordination of the group as a whole, while Handley Page acted as main contractor and provided assistance in the training of staff. A major problem was that the LAPG had no experience of aircraft production and it was therefore agreed that the first twenty sets of components would be assembled as a training exercise before the remaining ones were attempted. Also, in order to maintain a high standard of production, one aircraft from each hundred produced was to be flown to Handley Page's facility at Radlett for testing by pilots, with any necessary adjustments being reported back to LAPG. Protracted discussions between the various parties involved took place and the final go-ahead to assemble the Halifaxes was eventually given by the MAP on 31 March 1941. Luckily the Halifax had been designed on the split-construction principle, originated and developed by Handley Page, which divided the aircraft into major sections, each of which could be sub-divided and manufactured at dispersed shadow factories. This system was ideally suited to the inexperienced LAPG. Assembly at Leavesden eventually commenced in the number one factory in August 1941 from components supplied by the five members of the LAPG. Rear fuselages came from Chrysler Motors, front fuselages from Duple Bodies, fuselage and wing centre sections from LPTB (including two of the four engines), intermediate wings and tail units from Express Motors, and outer wings and engine cowlings from Park Royal Coachworks. Remaining elements were manufactured by LPTB, who also installed two of the Halifax's four engines. After many delays, the first LAPG-built Halifax, B Mk 2 BB189, finally took to the air on 8 December 1941 and was flown to Handley Page's airfield at nearby Radlett for flight-testing. A further 709 followed until the last, B Mk 3 PN640 *London Pride*, was rolled out on 16 April 1945 and took part in a fly-past and handing-over ceremony conducted by Lord Ashfield, chairman of both the LAPG and LPTB. This event was attended by hundreds of workers as well as Sir Frederick Handley-Page himself. During an earlier speech in December 1944, Lord Ashfield praised the work done by LAPG by saying, 'Five undertakings not previously associated in business and with no common link have been forged together into an effective production unit and have worked together in the closest harmony.' When a new LAPG-built Halifax was due for delivery, pilots would compete for it as they knew that it had come from the works that had formerly made London buses and would have seats covered in green leather to give additional comfort. They also had superior riveting, which was claimed to boost the airspeed by 10–15 knots. Of the 710 Halifaxes assembled at Leavesden, 450 were B Mk 2 variants with Rolls-Royce Merlin engines and 260 were B Mk 3s powered by Bristol Hercules radial engines. At the peak of production, some 4,600 staff were directly employed by the LAPG, of whom 80 per cent had no previous engineering experience and over half were women. The group comprised forty-one separate factories and over 600 sub-contractors. There are currently only two surviving Halifaxes in Great Britain, one in the RAF Museum, Hendon, and the other in the Yorkshire Air Museum at Elvington.

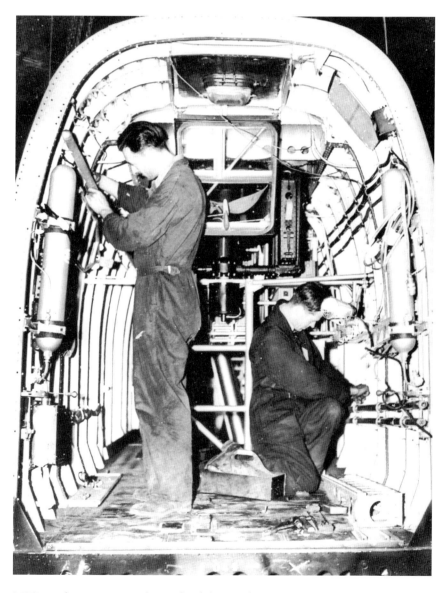

LPTB workers equipping the inside of the rear fuselage section of an LAP Halifax in September 1942. The man on the left is fitting a hand rail that runs the entire length of the fuselage. The two cylinders, one either side, are two of the four hydraulic accumulators. (*Rolls-Royce*)

Assembled Handley Page Halifax forward fuselage sections, minus the Boulton Paul nose gun turrets, at the London Passenger Transport Board's (LPTB) massive Aldenham premises at the bottom of Elstree Hill on the A41. (*Rolls-Royce*)

The centre-section of a Halifax being worked upon at the Aldenham works. Unlike the Lancaster fuselage, the Halifax fuselage was built in four sections and was constructed on the split-construction principle, which enabled subdivision and manufacture at dispersal factories. (*Rolls-Royce*)

A row of Rolls-Royce Merlin XX in-line water-cooled engines receiving attention at Aldenham before being installed into the awaiting Halifax centre-sections and outer wings. Of the 710 Halifaxes assembled at Leavesden, 450 were powered by Rolls-Royce Merlin in-line engines. The remainder were fitted with Bristol Hercules radial engines. (*Rolls-Royce*)

The flight engineer and radio operator's sections being worked upon by two of the many female staff at the Aldenham factory. The cylindrical pipe issuing from the bulkhead provided hot air from the two inner engines to the pilot. (*Rolls-Royce*)

A photograph of the front gun turret, taken before the two .303 Browning machine-guns have been fitted. The prone bomb-aimer's position in the Halifax demonstrates how cramped the space was for both occupants. (*Rolls-Royce*)

Wooden three-bladed constant-speed full-feathering Rotol propellers awaiting installation at the No. 1 Factory's Halifax assembly hall. (*Rolls-Royce*)

Will it fit? A starboard wing about to be mated to a Halifax in the No.1 Factory at Leavesden. The Halifax wing was built in five parts: a centre-section and two outer sections either side. (*Rolls-Royce*)

Rolls-Royce Merlin XX engines and accompanying cowlings are fitted to a Halifax II at the No. 1 Factory. (*Rolls-Royce*)

This Halifax has been pushed out and a last-minute inspection of the Rolls-Royce Merlin XX engines is taking place. Note the large one-piece aluminium forks of the backward retracting Messier undercarriage. Also note the Perspex blister just aft of the nose-turret – through which the navigator had a wide field of vision (*Rolls-Royce*)

A different view of the above. (*Rolls-Royce*)

A tired lady! A couple of Leavesden workers pretend to push a female colleague ensconced in a Halifax tyre. (*Rolls-Royce*)

A Halifax awaiting test-flying at Leavesden. Note the unpainted centre-section. (*Rolls-Royce*)

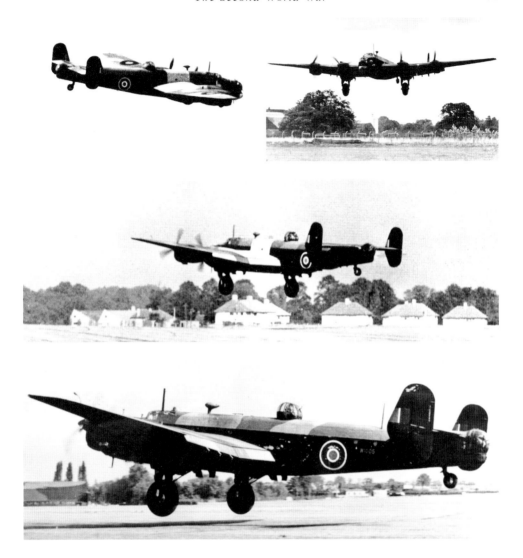

Views of English Electric-assembled Halifax II W1005 and possibly the first Leavesden-assembled aircraft (BB189 with unpainted centre-section) during demonstration flights at Leavesden in December 1941. Note the non-retractable tail wheel. The dorsal turret reportedly slowed the aircraft by some 10 mph. BB189 suffered an undercarriage collapse in March the following year, while landing at RAF Ricall in Yorkshire.

This publicity shot of a London bus and its driver and clippie taken at Leavesden gives some indication of the size of the Halifax IIs, which were 20 feet 9 inches high.

The last Leavesden-assembled Halifax, B Mk 3 PN 640 *London Pride*, awaiting delivery. Note the D-type fins and H2S radome.

A poor but interesting photograph taken in April 1944 of the all-white Halifax II JP301, destined for 58 Squadron (at that time transferred to Coastal Command). It would be used on anti-submarine patrols on the Western Approaches. This aircraft was part of a batch of 250 Leavesden-assembled Halifax IIs delivered between July 1943 and June 1944. (*E. J. Riding*)

Some of the workforce at Leavesden stand on, and in front of, perhaps the last Leavesden-assembled Halifax.

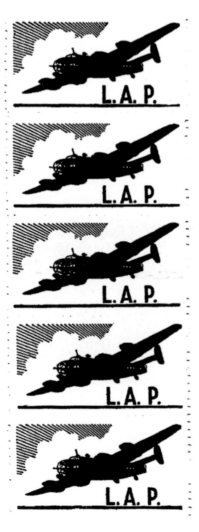

Albert Gent was a designer/draughtsman at the LPTB Aldenham works during the Second World War and designed these gummed labels to stick on Halifax drawings in order to distinguish them from bus drawings, which he also worked on. Some of the original labels are kept at the London Transport Museum, Covent Garden. (*Colin Gent*)

Above and below: Delightfully atmospheric views of knocking-off time at Leavesden. Note the Tilling-bodied open-staircase AEC Regents in the background, finally phased out on London streets in the 1940s. The bus services suffered problems in the early days due to the large workforce that had to be moved around; additional buses were provided to cope with the numbers.

A complete Halifax with Bristol Hercules radial engines outside No. 1 Factory *c*. 1943. Note the unfaired leading edges inboard of the engines, showing cable runs etc. (*Craig Woods*)

Air Transport Auxiliary

The Air Transport Auxiliary (ATA) was a civilian organisation set up at the outbreak of the Second World War to ferry military aircraft from the factories to airfields, thus releasing service pilots for active duties. In 1942, the ATA set up a four-engined training course for their ferry pilots at Leavesden using Halifax B Mk 2 BB191, the third one built by LAPG. Although it was based at Leavesden for conversion training, the short runway was not suitable for practice circuits and landings and the Halifax was therefore flown out to airfields with longer runways, such as Bovingdon, Bassingbourn and Hampstead Norris. The ATA school's instructor was a very experienced Polish pilot, Klemens Dlugaszewski, known as 'Dluga', who had been one of Poland's first commercial pilots, joining the Polish airline LOT at its foundation in 1929. Because of the shortcomings at Leavesden, the school moved to a more suitable site at RAF Pocklington in Yorkshire in February 1943. Lettice Curtis, the well-known ATA ferry pilot, remembers her conversion training at Leavesden and 'the 1,000-yard runway, one end of which sloped down towards the hangar where the Halifax was kept'. She was one of only a dozen or so female ATA pilots qualified to fly four-engined aircraft and went on to ferry numerous Halifaxes out of Leavesden and Radlett.

First Officer Ferdinand McDouall ATA, Algy Watson AID and First Officer 'John' Jordan ATA at Leavesden in April 1945. McDouall flew fighters in France and had broken his neck in a previous crash. 'John' Jordan was a member of the famous Jordans cereals family in Sandy, Bedfordshire, and in later life he owned and flew a Boeing Stearman in films and television, notably *Biggles*. (*E. J. Riding*)

ATA pilot and aviation artist Stanley Orton Bradshaw frequently gave ATC cadets from 2 and 3(F) Squadrons (Watford) air-experience flights in ATA Ansons. This photograph was taken on 18 August 1945 as twenty-one cadets prepared to board Avro Anson I NK810. (*E. J. Riding*)

ATC cadets of 2 and 3(F) Squadrons (Watford) prepare to board Avro Anson I EG228 on 22 September 1945 for an air-experience flight. Flown by Second Officer Stanley Orton Bradshaw ATA, the cadets were taken cloud-chasing 7,000 feet over London. EG228 was sold in 1950 and became G-AMBE on the British civil register and was eventually broken up for spares at Southend in 1962. (*E. J. Riding*)

ATA Anson I LT186 with Cheetah engines running. ATA cadets of 2 and 3 (F) Squadron (Watford) board for an air-experience flight with Stanley Orton Bradshaw at Leavesden on 13 October 1945. The last flight of that day, with a full load of cadets, lasted two hours and the route was: Gravesend and then Lympne, returning via Beachy Head, Gatwick and Staines. This particular Anson eventually passed to the Royal Hellenic Air Force in February 1947. (*E. J. Riding*)

ATA pilots First Officer Beatrice Hayman, First Officer Harry Guest and First Officer Cecil Hastings from South Africa at 'Leavesden Control' in May 1945. (*E. J. Riding*)

Between them these five ATA pilots ferried more than 5,000 aircraft to the RAF. Standing by a Mosquito 36 at Leavesden are, left to right, First Officers Richard Parnell, Harry Guest, Leslie Walton, Henry Stringer and Rowland Elliott. (*E. J. Riding*)

Mosquito Production

In early 1940, DH agreed to take on the building of Wellington bombers, but this was changed in 1941 to the production of its new Mosquito fighter/bomber aircraft popularly known as the 'Wooden Wonder'. DH accordingly set up a shadow factory at Leavesden called the Second Aircraft Group (SAG) for this purpose. This operation was based in the No. 2 Factory and drew components from more than 400 sub-contractors around the country, some of which had been commissioned originally to produce AW Albermarles. These ranged from coach builders and furniture manufacturers to small engineering companies and cottage industries, most of which had no previous experience of aircraft production. For example, fuselages were built at the Aldenham LPTB Works alongside Halifaxes, and wings were built at the Alliance factory on Western Avenue, Acton. The well-known furniture manufacturers E. Gomme Ltd (who made the G-Plan range), Parker Knoll, Waring & Gillow and Harris Lebus produced many wooden components. Birch logs from Canada were used for ply together with ash from nearby Whippendell Woods. When Mosquitoes were seen flying over Watford, it became a local custom to remark, 'There goes another piece of Whippendell Woods.' Metal parts and fittings, including many thousands of engine cowlings, were mostly produced at Greycaine's Printers in Bushey Mill Lane, Watford – which DH took over for the duration. In all the various production facilities, female labour played a vital part and made up about a third of the total labour force, working alongside men who had not been called up for military service. Prior to the Mosquito programme commencing, 140 sets of components for Airspeed Oxfords were produced together with a further sixty fuselages and 147 wings. Mosquito production then got underway, but in October 1941, when the first aircraft (T3 W4075) was nearing completion, the factory was still far from complete. It was rolled out in January 1942 and flown to Hatfield for flight-testing. Fifty-four examples were completed in 1942, 379 in 1943, 586 in 1944 and 371 in 1945, a total of 1,390, mostly trainer and night-fighter variants. Over 20 per cent of the wartime output of Mosquitoes took place at Leavesden and production continued until 1947. The last airworthy Mosquito in the UK was British Aerospace's T3 RR299, built at Leavesden in 1945 and a popular performer on the air-show circuit. Sadly it crashed during an air display at Barton Aerodrome, Manchester, on 21 July 1996, with the loss of the two crew members on board. There are currently about thirty surviving Mosquitoes in the world in varying degrees of restoration, of which seven are located in the UK. Unfortunately, none are airworthy.

Coastal Command Communication Flight

This flight was formed on 1 May 1944 at RAF Northolt and moved to Leavesden on 7 April 1945 as the Coastal Command Communication Squadron. It used a dozen aircraft, including the DH Dominie, Miles Master, Avro Anson, Airspeed Oxford, Percival Proctor and Lockheed Hudson, the latter being the personal mount of the AOC Coastal Command. The squadron disbanded on 1 May 1946 and eventually reformed at Bovingdon in July 1951.

A poor-quality photograph of an anonymous Airspeed Oxford taking off from Leavesden on 25 August 1945. E. J. Riding flew in Oxford V3598 on circuits and bumps on 22 June that year with Flt Lt Burroughs RAF. Various components for Oxfords were produced prior to the commencement of the Mosquito assembly programme. (*E. J. Riding*)

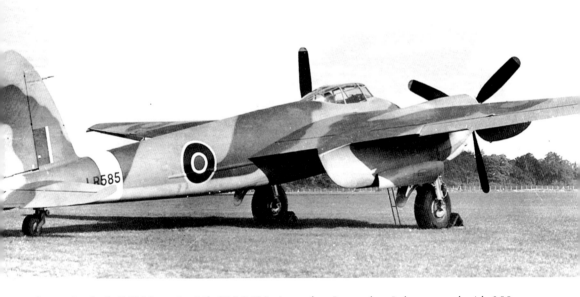

Leavesden-built DH Mosquito Mk III LR585 pictured at Leavesden. It later served with 255 Squadron at Kirton-in-Lindsey in 1944 before delivery to No. 1 Fighter Unit. This aircraft was from a batch of fifty-nine Mosquito Mk IIIs produced by Leavesden between December 1943 and December 1944. (*E. J. Riding*)

Three stages of Mosquito production at Leavesden, showing Mk NF-30s under production. In the foreground of the top photograph is NT435, initially delivered to 125 Squadron and eventually sold for scrap in July 1948. Between November 1944 and April 1945, Leavesden delivered 300 Mk NF-30s. (*BAE Systems*)

Above and below: Two views of Mosquito XIX MM652 taken at Leavesden in mid-1944. It flew with 157 and 169 Squadrons before being sold in Sweden *c.* 1948. It was one of a batch of fifty Mk XIXs constructed at Leavesden between April and May 1944. (*E. J. Riding*)

Mosquito XIII MM478 at Leavesden in early 1944 before delivery to 604 (County of Middlesex) Squadron at RAF Hendon. In March the following year, the aircraft came to grief while taxiing at Lille, France. MM478 was one of a batch of 141 Mk XIIIS delivered from Leavesden between February and May 1944. (*E. J. Riding*)

Mosquito NF-30 MV531 at Leavesden in late 1944. This short-lived aircraft was delivered to No. 1 Aircraft Delivery Flight at Hendon but crash-landed in a field in Surrey in October 1944. (*E. J. Riding*)

Mosquito NF-30 RK953 at Leavesden in May 1945. E. J. Riding and Freddie Offord made a forty-minute flight in this aircraft from Leavesden on 15 May 1945, when they 'shot up' Ruislip Lido, chased a Lancaster up to Leighton Buzzard, and tried to engage two Fairey Fireflies in mock combat over Aldenham – but the latter wouldn't play. RK953 was one of twenty-six Mosquito NF-30s rolled out at Leavesden between April and June 1945 and was delivered to 151 Squadron and sold as scrap in 1950. (*E. J. Riding*)

Production test pilot Freddie Offord could always be relied upon to make unorthodox returns from test flights. He often finished with a single-engine barrel roll. He is seen here in Mosquito NF-36 RL205 beating up Leavesden on one engine on 17 August 1945. (*E. J. Riding*).

On 17 August 1945, Mosquito NF-36 RL205 finally lands at Leavesden with both Merlins turning. (*E. J. Riding*)

A delivery line-up of Mosquito NF-36s pictured at Leavesden on the first day of peace: 17 August 1945. In the foreground is RL199, delivered to 85 Squadron. It later passed to the Station Flight at RAF Coltishall before being sold for scrap in January 1955. These Leavesden-built aircraft were part of a batch of 163 Mosquito NF-36s delivered between May 1945 and March 1947. (*E. J. Riding*)

Mosquito NF-36 RL232 at Leavesden in September 1945. E. J. Riding accompanied Freddie Offord on a jaunt to Panshanger and back on 8 September. At Panshanger, Offord gave a 'joyride' to an instructor and then beat up the place on leaving. This aircraft collided with NF-36 RK972 while landing at RAF Tangmere in April 1946. (*E. J. Riding*)

Mosquito NF-36 RL247 at Leavesden in September 1945. After being delivered to 228 OCU at RAF Leeming, this aircraft lost an engine while carrying out a forced landing near its base in March 1949. (*E. J. Riding*)

Above and below: Two photographs of the prototype Mosquito T-33 TS444 standing out in the wet on 1 February 1946, awaiting delivery to Boscombe Down for evaluation. The co-author's father, who was celebrating his thirtieth birthday on that day, accompanied Freddie Offord on this flight. But, on arrival, Boscombe Down didn't want it. After lunch the pair set off in rain and low cloud for the return flight to Leavesden but got lost. They ended up on the Kent coast and returned to Leavesden via Gravesend and Hornchurch. The flight to Boscombe took twenty-five minutes; the return flight forty-five minutes. (*E. J. Riding*)

E. J. Riding committing the dreadful sin of running up Mosquito T-III TV980 on it chocks with the tail wheel off the ground – a practice that was frowned upon for obvious reasons. TV980 was one of a batch of fifty T-IIIs delivered from Leavesden between July 1945 and May 1946. That same year TV980 was delivered to France's Armée de l'Air. (*E. J. Riding*)

The Leavesden Group's first Mosquito TR-33, TW227, pictured on 12 November 1945, two days after its first flight. This TR-33 was the first of the batch of 100 ordered from Leavesden in December 1944 and was delivered to the A&AEE on 16 November for handling trials. (*E. J. Riding*)

A line-up of Sea Mosquitoes destined for the Royal Navy at Leavesden on 4 December 1945. Note the deck-landing hooks beneath the tailplanes. These aircraft were delivered to Culham that same month and were part of an order for 100 TR-33s to be built at Leavesden. Ultimately only fifty were built and aircraft after TW239 – the aircraft pictured next to TW232 in the foreground – were cancelled. (*E. J. Riding*)

Above and below: Two photographs of Mosquito T-III TW241 at Leavesden in February 1946. E. J. Riding flew with a pilot named Storm Back from Leavesden to Hatfield and back on 21 February 1946. The comment in the remarks column in EJR's log book reads, 'Lunch at Hatfield.' The flights were ten minutes' duration each way. (*E. J. Riding*)

Test flights continued at Leavesden all through the winter months and here someone is seen clearing the snow away from the tailplane of Mosquito T-III TW241 prior to a test flight in February 1946. (*E. J. Riding*)

Mosquito T-III TW105, built for the Royal Navy, being prepared for flight at Leavesden in February 1946. EJR accompanied pilot Storm Back on the aircraft's first flight on 27 February. The forty-minute flight, in which the pilot let EJR have a go, included the beating up of Luton Airport. The aircraft was delivered to the Senior Service the following month. (*E. J. Riding*)

The lads and lasses of the Mosquito flight shed sit on and in front an example of their handiwork. John 'Tubby' Simpson and Freddie Offord are sitting fifth and sixth from left in the front row. (*E. J. Riding*)

Two RAF bods sitting in front of Mosquito NF-36 RK998 at Leavesden in mid-1945. After delivery to No. 23 Squadron, this aircraft was sold for scrap in March 1955. (*E. J. Riding*)

Flight-shed production foreman H. G. Harris, test pilot Freddie Offord, and flight-shed superintendent John 'Tubby' Simpson standing in front of Mosquito TR-33 TS449 at Leavesden in February 1946. On 5 February, Freddie Offord and EJR took this aircraft up to 14,000 feet and carried out four rolls and two loops with a half-roll out of each. Towards the end of the flight, Offord gave EJR some dual forced landing practice on a field near Sarratt just after take-off. (*E. J. Riding*)

Freddie Offord, production test pilot at Leavesden, photographed in Watford High Street *c.* 1946. Rumour has it that Offord returned to Canada after the war and broke his neck after falling down the stairs.

It's 1951 and some of the Leavesden staff are taking a break to make children's toys. An example of their professional handiwork stands in the background. (*BAE Systems*)

A break for a cuppa in one of the Leavesden workshops. (*BAE Systems*)

Lunchtime at Leavesden. Notice the number of people wearing ties and the odd worker or two still wearing his flat cap. (*BAE Systems*)

Enemy Action

Fortunately the aerodrome received only minimal attention from the enemy. On 2 October 1940 one high-explosive bomb landed about 300 yards from a flight-test hangar, which resulted in a crater some 50 feet wide and 3 feet deep. Nine days later, a number of high-explosive and oil incendiary bombs fell on the airfield, while on 20 October two high-explosive bombs landed, one of which did not explode. Finally, a number of high-explosive bombs were dropped on 2 December 1940, which resulted in four craters being made. Luckily none of these bombs caused any significant damage and there were no causalities. Curiously, the location for these attacks given in the Air Raid Precaution reports is 'Mile Field, Leavesden Green' – no mention is made of the airfield, but this was presumably for wartime security reasons.

Enemy aircraft were in the sky over Leavesden again on 23 September 1944 when a selection of captured German aeroplanes from No. 1426 Enemy Aircraft Flight (nicknamed the 'Rafwaffe') were flown into the aerodrome from their base at RAF Collyweston for display to the Royal Observer Corps (ROC). They included the Messerschmitt Bf 109 and 110 and the Junkers Ju 88. This event was attended by top brass from Fighter Command and the ROC. The main purpose of this flight was to familiarise aircrews with enemy aircraft, as well as for filming, sound recording, training and photographic purposes.

No.122 Elementary Gliding School (EGS)

In April 1946, this school moved to Leavesden from an unsatisfactory site at Northwick Park, Harrow, where it had been set up in October 1942. It operated Grunau Baby, Dagling Primary gliders and Kirby Cadets, which were launched by winch. F/O Green RAFVR (T) was initially its commanding officer at Leavesden, but was replaced by Flt Lt M. Purchase RAFVR (T). 122 EGS's stay at Leavesden was short-lived as it moved out in September 1947 and was homeless until February 1948, when it reformed at Halton. It eventually became No. 613 Volunteer Gliding School and is still going strong at RAF Halton.

USAAF Communications Flight

A small communications flight was set up by the USAAF at Leavesden in October 1944 under the command of Capt. R. Fowler and the aircraft used included three Fairchild C61s, one Cessna Bobcat and a Norduyn Norseman. Other pilots attached to the unit were Lt H. K. Sullivan, Capt. Talbot and Lt Owens.

Eddie Riding

E. J. Riding (EJR), co-author Richard Riding's father, worked as a Senior Aeronautical Inspection Directorate (AID) inspector at Leavesden from September 1943 until February 1946. Initially he was in charge of the No. 1 Flight shed and worked on pre-flight inspections on Halifaxes assembled by the LAPG in the No.1 Factory. Later, in June 1944, he was posted to the other side of the aerodrome to carry out similar work for the SAG, signing out several marks of Mosquito.

Coastal Command Communication Squadron Lockheed Hudson IIIA FK745 coming in to land at Leavesden on 8 August 1945. This aircraft saw service with 48 Squadron Coastal Command and ended up with the Air–Sea Warfare Development Unit and was finally taken off RAF charge in March 1948. (*E. J. Riding*)

Above and below: These poor quality photographs were taken on the occasion that No. 1426 Enemy Aircraft Flight of the RAF demonstrated some of its captured aircraft to the Royal Observer Corps (ROC) at Leavesden in September 1944. Above, ROC members inspect a captured Junkers Ju 88. Below, a Messerschmitt Bf 110 Werk No. 2177, which was allotted RAF serial AX772. Note the houses on Leavesden High Road in the background.

The USAAF at Leavesden. Douglas C-47B 43-49200 of the 9th Air Force in February 1945. The aircraft returned to the USA in August 1945 and later became N481F. It was destroyed in an accident in May 1975. (*E. J. Riding*)

USAAF Noorduyn Norseman 44-70377 takes off from Leavesden on 25 August 1945. This aircraft was delivered to the USAAF on 5 September 1944 and was shipped to the 8th Air Force in Europe on 9 October. After the war it took up Swedish registry as SE-AYW and on 25 September 1950 it crashed into Lake Sitasjaure and sank. (*E. J. Riding*)

Above and below: Formation flying with the USAAF's Leavesden-based Fairchild C-61 43-14489. Lt Owen flies the aircraft over nearby St Albans in October 1944. (*E. J. Riding*)

The first series of Halifaxes EJR worked on was a batch of 250 B Mk 2s (JN882–JP338) delivered between July 1943 and June 1944, powered by four Bristol Hercules XXII radial engines. The first aircraft he signed out was JN942, in which he flew on 8 September 1943 with T. W. Morton as pilot. After the war, Morton set up Croydon-based Morton Air Services Ltd, a charter airline that operated mainly DH Doves and Herons throughout Europe until the end of the 1960s. LAPG Halifaxes at this time were test-flown by Morton and a number of service pilots, including Flt Lt E. Sandberg of the Norwegian Air Force and Flt Lt A. D. Smith of the RAF. These pilots were only too pleased to have on board the person responsible for signing out the aircraft they were testing! EJR made no fewer than seventy flights in Halifaxes while attached to the LAPG. Some of his flights as 'observer' were first flights, but they were usually second, third and sometimes fourth re-flights. Reasons for a re-flight were numerous, more often than not as a result of aileron or elevator trimming, boost re-sets, throttle adjustments and so forth. Mixed in with testing the Mk 2s were RR Merlin XXII-powered Halifax B Mk 3s; EJR's first ride in one was in MZ283 on 4 April 1944, flown by Morton. This routine continued until June 1944, EJR's final Halifax outing being B Mk 3 MZ305 on a third re-flight, lasting fifteen minutes.

Less than two weeks later, EJR was transferred to the other side of the aerodrome, to No. 2 Factory, to sign out DH Mosquitoes, the first being MM696, flown by Sqn Ldr Jack Greenland, a production test pilot with the parent company. This aircraft was from a batch of 109 Mosquito NF-30s delivered between April and August 1944. The delivery pilots were either company or service pilots, but mostly ATA men and women. During this time EJR forged several long-lasting friendships with the latter and once flew with Lettice Curtis of the ATA on a Halifax delivery flight in July 1944 from Leavesden to No. 158 Squadron's home in Driffield, Yorkshire.

EJR flew mostly with DH test pilot Freddie Offord and his log book is full of interesting entries, as shown on the accompanying facsimiles. The initial test flight invariably lasted 35–50 minutes; re-flights lasted 10–30 minutes, depending on the work involved. In addition to test flights, EJR went on delivery flights to squadrons, usually with an ATA pilot.

From November 1944, the SAG started work on a further batch of Mosquito NF-30s, beginning with NT241. The first of this batch signed out by EJR was NT245, in which he flew on its delivery flight to No. 218 MU at Colerne, Wiltshire. Concurrently, the SAG was also turning out a batch of 50 T Mk 3s in the RR270–319 series, which included the ill-fated RR299 referred to on page 40. Other batches of Mosquitoes produced at Leavesden included 163 NF-36s (RK935–RL430) delivered between May 1945 and March 1947 – although many of these were cancelled at the end of the war as they were no longer required – and T3s and Mk 33s for the Royal Navy. EJR signed out many of these aircraft and amassed seventy flights in Mosquitoes.

Several Mosquitoes in which EJR flew later distinguished themselves in combat; one in particular deserves a mention here. On 8 August 1944, EJR and Flt Lt Martin flew a fourth re-flight in NF-30 MM792 as part of the contractor's handling trials. This aircraft was delivered to No. 219 Squadron and became one of the highest-scoring Mossies of the war. After the squadron had moved to Amiens, France, in October 1944, MM792 shot down two Junkers 88s on 29 November. On 26 December a Junkers 87 fell to its guns, followed by another in January 1945. A further Junkers 87 was shot down on 24 February 1945, but on 22 March the Mosquito's luck ran out when it went missing while on patrol.

```
                THE IDLE RICH.


     At Leavesden, home of L.A.P.,
     Exists a branch of A.I.D.,
     Which, in case you may forget
     Can be translated "All In Debt"?  Doubt ?
     Small wonder too, at our dilemma -
     We stop at half-past-six pip-emma.
     You'd think that with all our perfection
     We'd get as much as Works Inspection.
     Not so, dear friend, our credit's burst
     At ten A.M. on the thirty-first !.
     Our clothes are rags, our hat's a shell,
     We've got no shoes, so what the 'ell !.
     At Romney House, That Ancient Pile -
     Minus window, door and tile
     Sit A.I.D's most cherished sons -
     The S.I.O's and A.I.l's.
     It was from here in 'thirty-nine
     Went forth the order "Toe the Line -
     At beck or call, without a fight,
     At any hour of day or night".
     They used to rake us from our beds
    (Whereon we'd scarcely laid our heads)
     "We have a fuselage, Stage 3 -
     Outside awaiting A.I.D.".
     At two A.M. and sometimes three,
     They'd bring a lousy cup of tea -
     Their grateful thanks for overtime - free,
     That was the way in the A.I.D.
     Strangely enough in present days,
     The Ministry has got a craze
     To regulate our state of wealth
     In order to preserve our health !.
     Our brains and bodies, so they state
     Would be fatigued by working late,
     And so our hours each week we strive
     To keep within the fifty five.
     It's nice to think that P.A.2
     Concerns itself with what we do,
     But even so, in times of stress,
     Surely instead of working less
     We ought to make production rocket
     Without a bribe to fill our pocket;
     Far better if they'd subsidise
     A living wage of such a size
     That there wouldn't be a need
     Of graft and calculating greed
     In adding up the monthly score
     To see if youvcan make it more !.
     The moral's here for all to see -
     Wash out the bonus and O.T..
     We only ask to get our due,
     So pay us all a decent screw !.
```

'The Idle Rich' – an AID inspector's lament. Almost certainly penned by E. J. Riding while at Leavesden.

A Halifax flight-test crew with E. J. Riding (second from right) and John 'Tubby' Simpson (right). (*E. J. Riding*)

Buddies. Left to right: E. J. Riding AID and flight engineer John 'Tubby' Simpson pose in front of a Halifax at Leavesden. (*E. J. Riding*)

RECORD OF FLIGHTS. (1944)

Date.	Aircraft. Type.	Markings.	Engines. Type.	H.P.	Journey. From.	To.	Time of Departure. Hrs.	Mins.	Time of Arrival. Hrs.	Mins.	Time in Air. Hrs.	Mins.	Pilot. See Instructions (5) & (6) on flyleaf of this book.	Remarks.
						Brought forward	...	...	...	...	75	11.		
44.	H.P. 61. HALIFAX III	MZ.284	4. BRISTOL HERCULES XVI.		LEAVESDEN.	LUTON & BEDFORD.	17	40.	17	55.		15.	T. W. MORTON.	4th Re-flight. — BOOST ADJUSTMENTS. TRUMAN F/E. P. in MID UPPER.
44.	H.P. 59.	JP.324	4. R. R. MERLIN XXV		"	LINSLADE	16	25	16	45.		20.	"	3rd Re-flight. – Aileron Trim. TRUMAN F/E. CLOUD 3/10 4000ft. WIND N.W.
44.	H.P. 59. HALIFAX II	JP.331	"		"	MAR. 1R...	10	55	11	15		55	F/L H.L. SMITH.	1st re-flight via '3rd from ret via Milk VIA High Wycombe on Ret. 3,000 ft.
44.	"	JP.334	"		"	MARLOW	18	50	19	15.		25	"	ALT.10 M. AND N. 80-85 MPH. P/C JET. SERNE 2nd FLIGHT. MARK TO 7000'. REAR DOOR
44.	H.P. 61. HALIFAX III	MZ.295.	4. BRISTOL HERCULES XVI.		"	PRINCES RISBOROUGH	17	25	17	45.		20.	T. W. MORTON.	OPENED INDNE. WIND W. 5 MPH HOT. FZ. JET. 1st FLIGHT. 1500ft HI-CALL. VIA WHOLT
44.	"	MZ.297.	"		"	ESHER	16	10.	16	35		25	"	CALLED ESHER. DULL. 7/10 CLOUD. P/C SHAVE 2nd Flight. VIA W.DRAYTON Manor with 'FLIGHT
44.	"	MZ.303.	"		"	DOWNTON... MIDDONTON.	03	50	13	00		42	"	THUNDERBOLT D3'L. IN FORMATION. ROLLING ALONGSIDE & FLYING INVALIED
						Carried forward	...	...	...	...	78	40		

A double page from E. J. Riding's Flying Log Book recording just some of the seventy Halifax flights from Leavesden in which he was a passenger or 'observer'. Production test pilots were only too happy to have an AID inspector fly with them on test flights.

Relaxing in the Leavesden sun. Mosquito Mk III TV960 has just returned from a test flight in September 1945. Sitting on the tailplane is E. J. Riding. After delivery to 13 OTU at Bicester, TV960 was taken off RAF charge in June 1946. (*E. J. Riding*)

RECORD OF FLIGHTS. 1946.

Date.	Aircraft. Type.	Aircraft. Markings.	Engines. Type.	H.P.	Journey. From.	Journey. To.	Time of Departure. Hrs.	Mins.	Time of Arrival. Hrs.	Mins.	Time in Air. Hrs.	Mins.	Pilot. See Instructions (5) & (6) on flyleaf of this book.	Remarks.
						Brought forward	...	...	...		160	35		
.46.	D.H.98 MK.III.	TV.984	2 R-R. MERLIN 22.		LEAVESDEN.	LOCAL.	15	15	15	35		20.	S. F. OFFORD.	1ST TEST FLIGHT. TO 11,700'. WHITE SMOKE FROM 3 NO 3 JOINT.
.46.	D.H.98. MK.36.	RL.254.	2 R-R. MERLIN 114.		"	"	15	10	15	35.		25.	"	2ND. ½ CLOUD BASE 1500'. WIND UNIFORM-BLIZZARD + TRAIN SHOT JO.
.46.	D.H.98 MK.33.Ⓑ	TS.444	2 R-R. MERLIN 35		"	BOSCOMBE DOWN.	10	30	10	55.		25.	"	DELIVERY FLIGHT TO AI AEE. VIA ANDOVER + SALISBURY. — B.D. 718 LOST IN RAIN + LOW CLOUD. ENDED C
.46.	"	TS.444.	"		BOSCOMBE DOWN.	LEAVESDEN.	15	25.	16	10		45.	"	KENT COAST. BACK VIA GRAVESEND + HO TO 14,000'. 4 ROLLS + 2 LOOP
.46.	D.H.98 MK.III.	TW.103.	2 R-R. MERLIN 21.		LEAVESDEN.	LOCAL.	11	25	12	00.		35	"	✗SCROLL OUT. CL'G. TO 14,200'. DIV 1ST FLIGHT. INSTRUCTION. —
.46.	D.H.98 MK.36.	RL.258.	2 R-R. MER. 114.		"	"	11	00.	11	45.		45.	STORM BACK	TURNS + LANDING APPROACH 1ST TEST. 3. LAYERS OF CLOU
.46.	D.H.98. MK.3.	TW.103.	2 R-R. MERLIN 21.		"	"	15	15.	15.	35.		20.	"	2ND. DUAL. — TURNS LANDING APPROACH.
							11	55.	12	25.		30		
						Carried forward	...	...	...		104	40		

RECORD OF FLIGHTS. 1945.

Date.	Aircraft. Type.	Aircraft. Markings.	Engines. Type.	H.P.	Journey. From.	Journey. To.	Time of Departure. Hrs.	Mins.	Time of Arrival. Hrs.	Mins.	Time in Air. Hrs.	Mins.	Pilot. See Instructions (5) & (6) on flyleaf of this book.	Remarks. EPPING. THEN VIA RADLET
						Brought forward	155	25.	...		153	25.		CHASED LANC. TO MILDENH
9.11.45.	D.H.98. MK.33.	TW.230.	2 R-R. MERLIN 29s.		LEAVESDEN.	—	14	25	15	10		45	S. F. OFFORD.	SHOT HIM 4 TIMES LOW FLY TO HATFIELD TO COLLECT
"	"	"	"		"	HATFIELD.	16	40	16	45		05	"	LOCKING FLAPS. —"DUSK. LIGHTS ON IN ST ALBANS
"	"	"	"		HATFIELD.	LEAVESDEN.	16	50	16	55		05	"	LAMPS ON RUNWAY. SPEEDS @ 14+31,000'. DI
14.11.45.	"	"	"		LEAVESDEN	LOCAL.	11	10	11	50		40	"	OVER LUTON (270 KNOTS + 3½ DIVE ON EATON BRAY. — STOP
17.11.45.	D.H.98. MK.36 NF.	KL.246.	2 R-R. MERLIN 114.	1,850.	"	"	11	30.	11	55		25	"	3M. IN FEATHER. — PINE ENGINE COURSE 06°. DIVE FR.6,000'.
26.11.45.	D.H.98 MK.33.	TW.231.	2 R-R. MERLIN 25		"	"	15	40	16	10		30	"	HALF RU-½ INSTONE. SHOT EATON B RE-FLIGHT AFTER PITING DECK HOOK.
19.12.45.	"	TW.235.	"		"	"	14	30.	15	00.		30.	"	1500 GLO. 140'OUT'. ½ WALTING CHASED SILVER WHIFFET BEHIND BAR
5.1.46.	"	TW.233.	"		"	"	11	40	12	15		35	"	TO 15,000'. — CL'G. ½ ROLLS. — OUT OF CLOUD @ 2,000' 0·15L REATE FLEW 'ROUND' MILES 'HEROVAN
						Carried forward	...	...	...		156	55		MK·I PROP FEATHERED RECORD ·1 415.1·1 +·2 MM·2·5."

Typical double-page entries from E. J. Riding's flying log book during his time signing out Leavesden-built Mosquitoes, including the abortive trip to Boscome Down in Mosquito TR-33 prototype TS444. E. J. Riding had forty-two hours' airborne time in seventy Leavesden-built Mosquitoes between June 1944 and February 1946

And now for something completely different. E. J. Riding was a prolific scale-aircraft modeller and produced a dozen or so models for *Aeromodeller* magazine. One of his early models was the Bristol Scout. Initially rubber-powered but later fitted with a diesel engine, it was flight-tested inside the Mosquito flight shed before further tests were made outside. This picture and the one that follows were taken at Leavesden in the autumn of 1945 and published in the Christmas 1945 edition of *Aeromodeller* with a colour cover painting by aeronautical artist C. Rupert Moore, a personal friend of E. J. Riding, whose Radlett studio was often the target for low-flying Mosquitoes flown by Freddie Offord and Co. (*E. J. Riding*)

In this picture, C. Rupert Moore is about to launch the Bristol Scout for a flight test at Leavesden. (*E. J. Riding*)

The original painting by C. Rupert Moore used on the front cover of the Christmas 1945 edition of *Aeromodeller*.

Three photographs of Leavesden and the immediate vicinity taken by
E. J. Riding from the dorsal turret of Halifax II JP193 while returning
to the Leavesden circuit on 6 January 1944, flown by T. W. Morton.
Note the Mosquitoes awaiting testing and delivery in the bottom
photograph. (*E. J. Riding*)

Production test-flying and delivery flights had their more exciting and lighter moments. On 28 July 1945, Freddie Offord and EJR took off from Leavesden in Mosquito Mk 36 RL152 and headed for France. They hit the French coast at St Jouin-sur-Mer, a small seaside village nestling between the cliffs, and flew along the coast at zero feet to Etratat, where they 'beat up' the jetty while a leave train was alongside it. They then headed out to sea at 100 feet all the way, arriving back at Leavesden ninety-five minutes later. Offord had a reputation for concluding his production test flights by performing barrel rolls with one or both engines feathered!

Another jaunt with Offord beggars belief. They literally went to see a man about a dog. On 31 August 1945, he and EJR left Leavesden in Mosquito Mk 36 RL231 and landed at Staverton Aerodrome near Gloucester, where Offord had arranged to meet a man who wanted to sell an Alsatian pup. The pup turned out to be a four-year-old and stood 'as high as a small pony'. With much pulling and hauling, they managed to get the dog into the cockpit and lashed it to the radar-scanner crate. They expected a blood bath when the engines were started, but the dog settled into what EJR later described as a sort of coma and just laid on the floor and dribbled. To make matters worse, the pilot got lost on the return journey and it was only after he got his bearings from the radio station at Rugby that he was able to fly back to Leavesden. The dog, surely the only canine to take a ride in a Mosquito, was none the worse for the trip.

The following anecdotes are recorded in letters from EJR to A. J. Jackson, the well-known aviation historian:

21 June 1943

Last Saturday pm was the epitome of bliss. I had a ride in Halifax Mk.2 HR921. It lasted 50 minutes and we went down beyond Reading almost as far as Newbury. I climbed into the dorsal turret after take-off and stayed there until asked to go forward for the trimming trials, finishing up in the bomb-aimer's seat in the nose. It was a lovely day and we skimmed down valleys of clouds taking some like hurdles and ploughing through the big ones. There were only three of us on board, including the pilot Sqn. Ldr. Mitchell. Only one complaint – it was too darned hot. I sat up in my 'bird cage' roasting slowly. They ought to put ventilators in these kites.

28 September 1943

Last Monday I had a real five bob one. Halifax JN960 was the hearse and we went up as far as the suburbs of Birmingham and back. Most of it was above cloud and the scenery up there was really grand. I sat in the dorsal turret all the time and was thrilled to the marrow watching a Beaufighter creep to within 200 ft of the tailplane and then proceed to cut us up and generally demonstrate that we were standing still.

We had a dinghy blow out over Aylesbury last week. It hasn't been found yet and I guess said dinghy is probably making admirable hot water bottles for the yokels for miles around.

22 October 1943

Have just had another very fine trip; one hour in Halifax JN111. We cruised backwards and forwards between Hemel Hempstead and Leighton Buzzard. After the testing was over we hied down to Heathrow and beat them up and were 'attacked' by a Polish Spitfire from Northolt. He flew alongside and made rude gestures and then did mock attacks from the rear.

28 June 1944

Since a week last Thursday we have been showered with devices called Fly-bombs, Buzz-bombs, Kivik rockets or, to put it in the words of a certain gentleman at work, 'Blarstards', which I think describes them to a 'T'. We average 10 or 12 daytime alerts and the usual all night session until 4am. So, for 'Southern England' read the usual target and you won't be far wrong. Until this am we'd had nothing within one and a half miles but I gather that 'some damage and casualties have occurred elsewhere'. They sound like Trojan vans in flight and when the propulsion unit starts coughing you look around for a convenient hole and pull it in after you. Flying speed appears to be in the neighbourhood of 350 mph and the stalling speed 330 mph. Result – straight in – bonk. The plumbers will no doubt be busy putting a few windows back when the originators run out of ammo. I saw one shot down by a Spitfire Vb over Harrow last week. The censor seems to be opening several outgoing letters recently – a woman down the road mentioned in a letter to her husband that she was 'sitting in the garden during an alert writing this letter' and they sent it back to her.

27 September 1944

Went across to the old firm (LAP) yesterday and bought a ticket for a Halifax ride. Only 20 minutes to Henley and back but it made a change from the usual streamlined bricks (Mosquitoes). We've had three prangs and two near misses over that trouble I told you about.

Jim Mollison's been in twice – he's getting fatter and you'd hardly recognize him.

CHAPTER THREE

POST-WAR DEVELOPMENTS

The End of the War

With the coming of peace, Halifax production came to an end and an outstanding contract for 120 aircraft was cancelled. Work on the Mosquito continued in a low key for a further couple of years. The considerable wartime activity on the site paved the way for its subsequent use; the LAPG terminated its occupation of No.1 Factory and the premises were given care-and-maintenance duties while DH took over the SAG's No. 2 Factory for its own use. In September 1945, Watford Borough Council wisely decided to secure future employment for thousands of local people and recommended the Ministry of Defence grant a lease to the DH Company to enable aircraft and engine production to continue at Leavesden.

The DH Engine Division

The Engine Division of the DH Aircraft Company produced its first successful commercial engine in 1927, the four-cylinder Gipsy of 135 hp, which was introduced to power the Moth series of aircraft. The Engine Division operated as part of the parent company until 1 February 1944, when a separate engine company was formed at Stag Lane, Edgware. Before the Second World War, the company's main focus had been on the Gipsy piston engine series, which powered light aircraft and small airliners with outputs of 90–525 hp, which was adequate at the time. The Engine Division produced 10,212 examples during the war years alone, and also overhauled over 9,000 Rolls-Royce Merlin engines between 1940 and 1944. However, in April 1941, priorities changed when the Air Ministry awarded a contract to the Engine Division for the development of a turbojet engine based on the successful results of Frank Whittle's research. In order to make progress, a consultant, Maj. Frank Halford, was engaged by DH to take charge of it. (Halford had earlier consulted on the Gipsy engine.) A year later, in April 1942, the first prototype Halford H-1, later named Goblin, was test-run. The following year it powered the second prototype of the first British jet fighter, the Gloster Meteor, and then the DH Vampire. This success secured the future of the company and in July 1943 a prototype Goblin was shipped to the USA to power Lockheed's P80 Shooting Star. Around this time, DH purchased Halford's company and set him up as chairman and technical director of its Engine Division. Over 5,000 Goblin engines were built in the United Kingdom and under licence abroad. In 1946 the production of Gipsy and Goblin engines was moved from Edgware to the Leavesden No. 1 Factory. Sheet-metal fabrication

Vickers Wellington XIV MF639 at Leavesden on 17 September 1945. It bears the code letters 'NH' of 38 Squadron. Built at Squires Gate, Blackpool, this Wellington served with the Leigh Light Training Unit until it was struck off RAF charge in 1947. (*E. J. Riding*)

Weather-beaten Saro-built Supermarine Walrus I L2251 at Leavesden on 17 September 1945. Before the war, this amphibian was based with 'D' Flight at RNAS Ford. (*E. J. Riding*)

Avro Anson I G-AHUD at Leavesden on 8 July 1947. Previously LT766 with the RAF, this Anson was registered to British American Air Services in June 1946. Its Certificate of Airworthiness had lapsed by 1949. (*E. J. Riding*)

for DH engines was relocated from the company's wartime home at Greycaine's Printers to Stonegrove and also the No. 2 Factory, after Mosquito production had been completed. DH then started to make significant progress in the aerospace industry, initially with the Ghost engine, the worthy successor to the Goblin, in 1947. This engine powered the world's first jet airliner, the DH Comet, as well as the DH Venom and SAAB J29 fighters. It was the world's first jet engine certified for passenger service.

By 1953, the Gyron had evolved. It was the most powerful jet engine in the world at that time. It was intended to power the Avro 730 supersonic bomber and the Hawker P1121 interceptor, but both these projects were cancelled in April 1957 as a result of a Government White Paper that recommended the phasing-out of conventional aircraft in favour of missiles. The Gyron was briefly test-flown in a Short Sperrin bomber from Hatfield in 1955 and ultimately produced greater thrust than any known engine at that time. Ironically a similar engine was developed by the Russians and became the Tumansky R266, which powered the successful MiG 25 Fox Bat. With the performance of the Gyron proven, DH took the decision to develop a three-fifths-scale version known as the Gyron Junior. This engine was first test-run in August 1955 and was selected to power the Blackburn NA39 naval strike aircraft, later to become the Buccaneer, which first flew in April 1958. The Gyron Junior was further developed into a smaller-scale version known as the PS50, which in 1962 briefly powered the ill-fated Bristol 188 high-speed research aircraft. It was also intended for the Saunders-Roe 177 high-altitude interceptor, but this never flew. In March 1954, Leavesden became the head office of the DH Engine Company with the Engineering Division at Stag Lane and the Test and Research centre at Hatfield.

An undated photograph of Sir Geoffrey de Havilland at Leavesden about to press the starter of a replica of his first engine, produced by Leavesden apprentices. The original engine was a four-cylinder flat engine that gave around 40 hp. It weighed 250 lb, of which 27 lb was the flywheel. (*BAE Systems*)

Mr. Turner, one of the instructors in charge of the building of the replica engine, is seen supervising an apprentice working on one of the cylinder cooling jackets. Note the DHAETS Engines motif on the apprentice's overalls. (*BAE Systems*)

A supercharged direct-drive de Havilland Gipsy Major 51 engine that gave 195 hp take-off power.

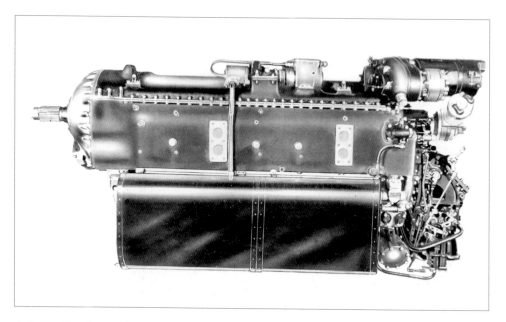

A de Havilland supercharged Gipsy Queen 71 engine. It gave 330 hp take-off power.

A view of No. 1 Factory with Gipsy engine production in full swing in 1948. The Process Shop can be seen top left. (*Rolls-Royce Heritage Trust*)

Leavesden's No. 2 Factory, *c.* 1950. Note the 'Stage 11' sign on the far wall, a leftover from the days of Mosquito production. (*BAE Systems*)

Instructor Ray Thomas, centre, with apprentices Colin A. Smith, left, and Steve Turner lifting a de Havilland Goblin turbojet from its stand. (*BAE Systems*)

Opposite, above: The first of the series of de Havilland gas turbine engines was the Goblin turbojet, seen here with Maj. Frank B. Halford (centre), chairman and technical director of the de Havilland Engine Company Ltd. Left is E. S. Moult, who started with the company in 1927 and was its chief engineer. John L. P. Brodie, then in charge of the Engineering Division, is on the right. These three men created the Gipsy engine range and the first series of de Havilland Goblin turbines. (*BAE Systems*)

The De Havilland Goblin turbine. Tests began on the prototype Goblin in April 1942 and by March 1943 it was flying in a Gloster Meteor. In September, the prototype Vampire began flying with the Goblin and an example was installed and flown in the Lockheed Shooting Star prototype. By the spring of 1944, both the Meteor and the Shooting Star were exceeding 500 mph, the first aircraft in Britain or America to do so. In January 1945, the Goblin became the first turbine to achieve official type-approval and became the holder of Type Certificate No. 1. (*BAE Systems*)

Checking a de Havilland Goblin at the Leavesden factory – note the pin striped trousers!

The de Havilland Ghost (top) and the de Havilland Goblin (bottom). More than 5,000 DH Goblins were built in the UK and under licence abroad.

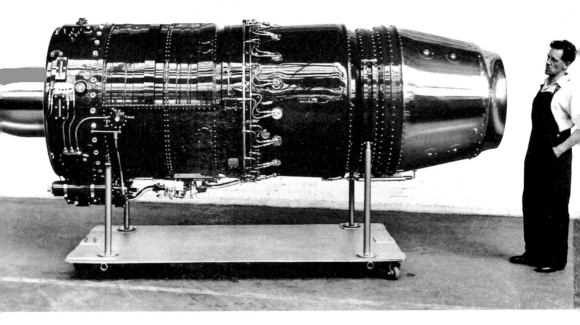

In 1953 the Gyron was the most powerful jet engine in the world.

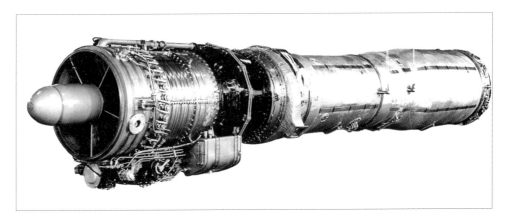

DH Gyron Junior PS 50 with reheat for the Bristol 188. The first of two flying examples of the Bristol 188, XF923, was first flown on 14 April 1961 and made its first public appearance at the 1962 SBAC show at Farnborough.

As well as competing in the jet- and piston-engine fields, a rocket-propulsion section was established in 1946. Over the next decade this produced some significant engines including the Sprite, Super Sprite and Spectre, which were mainly developed for use in assisting the take-off of heavily loaded aircraft, as well as powering the Saunders-Roe SR53 research aircraft and Blue Steel stand-off bomb. The responsibility for first run and subsequent development testing of all new engines was carried out at the DH test establishment at Manor Road, Hatfield, where some 140 personnel were employed. These test beds were to remain in use until June 1990. The engine company was no stranger to licence arrangements with other manufacturers and in 1966 an agreement was reached with the General Electric Company of the USA to manufacture the latter company's T64 free-turbine engine, but in the event this did not proceed. In August 1967, the Engineering Department vacated Stag Lane and all efforts were then located at Leavesden.

The DH Spectre rocket engine. The ill-fated Saunders-Roe SR-177 would have used this engine in combination with a DH PS 50 Gyron Junior.

A de Havilland Double Spectre.

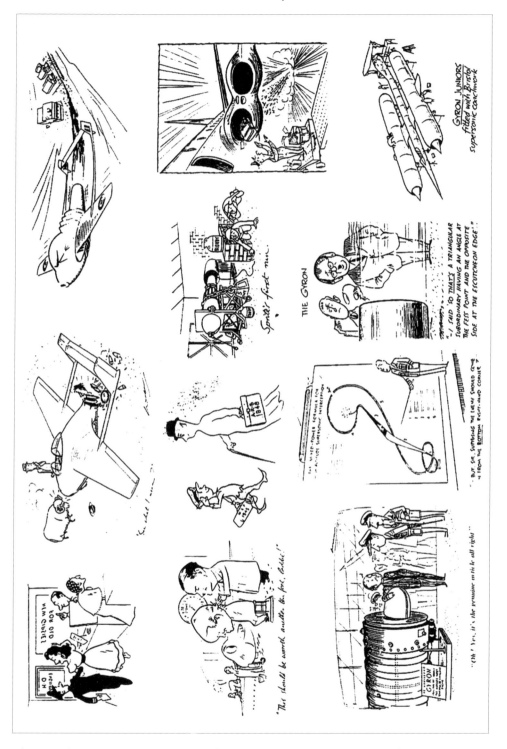

The Aeroplane's Chris Wren produced these cartoons showing the output of the de Havilland engine company. Of particular interest is the portrayal of de Havilland's chief test pilot having his hair cut; the caption reads, 'This should be worth another ten feet, laddie!'

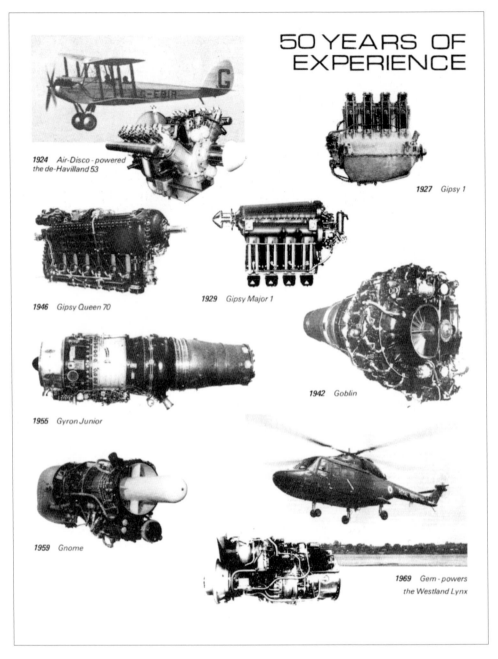

50 YEARS OF EXPERIENCE

1924   Air-Disco-powered the de-Havilland 53

1927   Gipsy 1

1946   Gipsy Queen 70

1929   Gipsy Major 1

1942   Goblin

1955   Gyron Junior

1959   Gnome

1969   Gem-powers the Westland Lynx

A poster charts the engines produced at Stag Lane and Leavesden, from the 1924 Airdisco-powered DH 51 (not 53, as stated here) to the 1969 Gnome-powered Westland Lynx.

The de Havilland Engine Company's showroom at Leavesden, showing an array of the company's products. Note the legendary DH 88 Comet G-ACSS *Grosvenor House* hanging from the ceiling in the background.

Expansion

With East and West in the grip of the Cold War and the start of the Korean War, DH predicted the need for additional military aircraft in order to increase Britain's defence capability. The DH Engine Company accordingly embarked on a major expansion at both Leavesden factories in anticipation of large orders for engines. This coincided with a move in 1954 from the Stonegrove works, which had been set up in 1944 to produce Goblin engines. At the same time, DH built a new administration block with a modern control tower on top. This exercise paid off, because sometime later the peak of around 4,800 employees was reached. Earlier, in 1951, enlargement of the airfield itself was considered as highly impracticable by the Ministry of Supply owing to the configuration of the ground outside the boundary, which sloped away to the west and south as well as having houses and a factory to the east and north.

Helicopter Engines

DH first became involved in rotary machines in 1931 with the Cierva C24 Autogyro G-ABLM, which was powered by a Gipsy III engine. (This aircraft is preserved at the de Havilland Heritage Museum at London Colney, Hertfordshire.) As a result of the loss of military contracts following the 1957 Defence White Paper, DH turned its attention to developing gas turbine engines for helicopters using its own in-house design/engineering and testing departments. Since the early 1940s, the company had enjoyed reciprocal agreements with the General Electric Company in the USA and in 1958 an agreement was signed for licensed production of the T58 turboshaft engine, which was in an advanced stage of development following a US Navy-sponsored programme. In June 1959, the Gnome derivative of this engine was tested in a Westland Whirlwind and this evolved into a turboshaft of 1,200 hp, which went on to power the Westland Wessex, Vertol 107, various SRN hovercraft and, later, the Sea King.

Above and below: Two views of the new administration building and control tower under construction in 1953. (*BAE Systems*)

A 1954 aerial view of the new control tower and associated buildings. (*BAE Systems*)

A view of new control tower in 1956. (*BAE Systems*)

As a result of amalgamations in the aircraft industry, the existing Blackburn gas turbine engines – derived from the French manufacturer Turbomeca – were absorbed by Bristol Siddeley engines from 1961 and further developed. These included the Nimbus, which powered the Westland Scout and Wasp from 1963. A later collaboration took place with Turbomeca in 1967, when a Memorandum of Understanding was signed by the French and British governments for joint production of three helicopter types and their engines: Gem, Turmo and Astazou. These powered respectively the Lynx, the Puma and the Super Frelon, and the Gazelle. Rolls-Royce, as the successor to Bristol Siddeley, went on to produce thousands of helicopter engines, including the RTM322 for the Merlin and the MTR390 for the Tiger, together with Palouste and Artouste auxiliary power units (APUs).

The importance of the helicopter-engine production facility at Leavesden can be measured by Rolls-Royce's appearance on a list prepared by MI5 of the top-ten IRA targets at the height of the latter's bombing campaign on the UK mainland.

A Bristol Siddeley Coupled Gnome H 1200 installed in a Westland Wessex 2 at Leavesden. It comprised two Gnome H 1200 engines driving through a common gearbox. (*BAE Systems*)

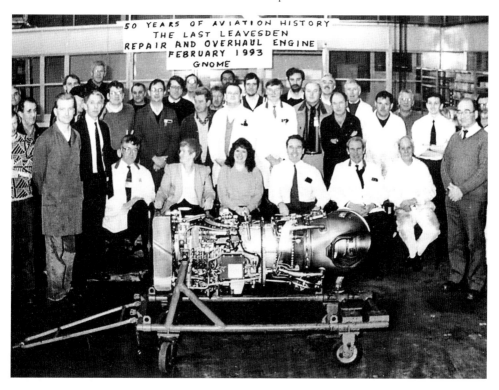

Above and below: Two photographs record the last Gnome engine overhauled at Leavesden in 1993. (*Craig Woods*)

The first RTM322 engine being worked on at No. 1 Factory. (*Craig Woods*)

A Gnome for a Wessex was the very last engine produced by Rolls-Royce at Leavesden, in February 1993. (*Craig Woods*)

Westland Whirlwind HAR 3 XJ398 of the Royal Navy hovers in front of the Leavesden control tower *c.* 1958. This helicopter has been preserved and is with the Yorkshire Helicopter Preservation Group at Doncaster. (*Craig Woods*)

An HKP-4 Vertol 107 of the Swedish Navy used for anti-submarine duties, at Leavesden. It was powered by two Leavesden-built Bristol-Siddeley Gnome H 1200 turbines. The Vertol 107 led to the Model 114, better known as the Chinook. (*Colin Morris*)

Sikorsky S 70C Blackhawk G-RRTM at Leavesden *c*. 1986. It was powered by two Rolls-Royce Turbomeca RTM322 engines. (*Craig Woods*)

Agusta Bell AB 204B I-AGUG at Leavesden *c*. 1966. (*Colin Morris*)

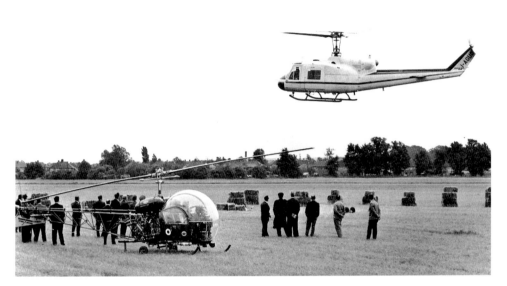

Agusta Bell AB 204B I-AGUG at Leavesden with an Army Air Corps Bell 47 Sioux *c.* 1966. (*Colin Morris*)

An anonymous Westland Wessex hovering in front of the tower. It was powered by two Leavesden-built Bristol Siddeley Gnome H 1200 free-turbine engines. (*Colin Morris*)

Army Air Corps Saro Skeeter AOP 12 XM527 at Leavesden *c.* 1959. It was later relegated to an instructional airframe: 7820M. Used for light-duty liaison work, the AOP 12 was powered by the Leavesden-built de Havilland Gipsy Major.

Saro P 531 Mk 1 G-APNU at Leavesden on 5 September 1958. The progenitor of the Wasp and Scout series, this five-seat aerodynamic prototype first flew in July 1958. Powered by a Blackburn-Turbomeca Turmo de-rated to 325 shp, G-APNU was withdrawn from use in 1960 and scrapped in 1972. (*Craig Woods*)

Faith in the Leavesden-built Bristol Siddeley Gnome H 1200 turbine could not be better demonstrated than by this view of Westland Wessex HCC 4 XV733 of the Queen's Flight. (*Craig Woods*)

The DH Aircraft Company

In 1946 a service department for DH civil aircraft was set up and later, in 1949, DH's entire repair, servicing and salvage operation moved in from Witney, Oxfordshire, occupying the No.1 Flight Shed at the western end of the runway. The department dealt initially with a variety of DH Company aircraft and then concentrated on Doves, Devons and Herons. Scores of these types passed through the workshop, some of which belonged to the rich and famous – who had contracts arranged for regular maintenance. When required, mobile teams were flown out to destinations all over the world to repair or service DH aircraft *in situ*. The last DH Aircraft Company military activity at Leavesden, in 1949, was the conversion of several Vampire aircraft in the No. 2 Factory for the Fleet Air Arm's rubber mat recovery-at-sea system. This involved the fitting of strengthened undersides to the aircraft in order to cope with landings on rubber mats with undercarriage retracted. At the same time, the No. 1 Flight Shed was used as a clearance/test facility for new Vampires and Venoms constructed by DH at nearby Hatfield. The DH Aircraft Company ceased its civil repairs at Leavesden in 1963 but continued this work in its factory at Hawarden, Chester. The last aircraft to receive attention at Leavesden was a Heron for the Royal Navy.

Left and below: Two views of DHC-3 Otter G-ANCM in No. 1 Flight Shed at Leavesden in 1953. This aircraft was built in Canada and shipped to Leavesden, where it was assembled and then flown as a European demonstrator in the hands of DHC's chief test pilot, George Neal. In 1957 the aircraft was sold to the Indian Air Force and became IM-1057. Since retirement from the IAF, the Otter has been preserved in the museum at Kalaikunda Air Base, 70 miles west of Calcutta. Foreman 'Ollie' Wood is standing on the ladder and Norman Eastaff is above the prop. (*Bruce McLeod*)

Above and below: Two views of the much-travelled DHC-3 Otter XL710, acquired for use for the 1956 British Commonwealth Trans-Antarctic Expedition. Following RAF service, the aircraft was handed over to the US Navy and then passed to the Royal New Zealand Air Force. Flown to Canada in 1964, it crashed in 1974. After sale to the USA, the Otter was rebuilt and registered N63535 in Washington in 1997. It survives there to this day. (*Craig Woods*)

Royal Navy de Havilland Dominie HG713 pictured at Leavesden in May 1952. Built by the Brush Coachworks in 1943, HG713 flitted around various naval stations until 1957. On 14 May 1952, the aircraft was damaged after landing and was taken to Leavesden and repaired, probably when this photograph was taken. The Dominie was scrapped in July 1963. (*John Bellam*)

A poor-quality photograph of the de Havilland Engine Company's DH 104 Dove G-AJGT in front of the control tower at Leavesden, *c.* 1955. It was broken up in 1979.

Above and below: Two views of an unidentified Royal Navy DH 114 Heron at Leavesden in 1963. This was the last aircraft to receive attention by de Havilland's Civil Repair Organisation. (*BAE Systems*)

Amalgamations and Takeovers

Since the end of Second World War the DH Engine Company had been in competition with other major aero-engine manufacturers such as Rolls-Royce, Bristol Siddeley, (formed by the merger in 1959 of Armstrong Siddeley and Bristol Engine Company) and Blackburn, but as a result of the early Comet 1 disasters, the 1957 White Paper, and competition from abroad (mainly the USA), a takeover was inevitable. This came in November 1961, when DH was acquired by Bristol Siddeley Engines and from 1965 became the Small Engine Division of this company. Blackburn Engines had already been taken over by Hawker Siddeley in 1959. (In late 1959, the de Havilland Aircraft Company became part of the Hawker Siddeley Group) At this time 3,600 people were employed at Leavesden, a considerable drop from the peak of 4,800 a decade earlier. A further reorganisation took place in October 1966 when Rolls-Royce took over Bristol Siddeley and centralised its small gas-turbine-engine work at Leavesden. Yet another change occurred in February 1971, when Rolls-Royce Ltd became bankrupt as a result of the crippling development costs of the RB211 engine intended to power the new breed of wide-body airliners. However, in May 1971, a new company, Rolls-Royce (1971) Ltd, emerged from receivership and this changed again to Rolls-Royce plc following a public flotation in 1985. Rolls-Royce at Leavesden produced engine parts for the RB211 (Tristar, Boeing 747 and 757 etc.), RB199 (Tornado) and Olympus 593 (Concorde). In 1980 the company developed the RTM322 engine jointly with Turbomeca of France to power the EH101 helicopter – now known as the Merlin – and the MTR390 for the Tiger helicopter. The Ministry of Defence put the airfield up for sale in June 1974 as they considered it surplus to defence needs. Both Rolls-Royce and Watford Borough Council expressed interest in buying it, Rolls-Royce to continue its operations and Watford Council to use it for housing. Fortunately nothing came of this proposal, and Rolls-Royce eventually purchased Leavesden from the MoD in 1990.

CHAPTER FOUR

GENERAL AVIATION

Development as a Commercial Airport

In 1959, the DH Engine Company began developing Leavesden as a commercial
airport, chiefly for the executive operator. This was to be an important role for
the next four decades. It was continually licensed by the Board of Trade until
September 1972, when this function was taken over by the Civil Aviation Authority
(CAA), and continued to be a licensed aerodrome until 31 October 1993. For the
remaining five months of its life it was unlicensed. It was fully equipped with some
of the most advanced navigational and landing aids and the concrete runway was
provided with lighting for night operations. In 1968 it had one concrete runway
3,281 feet long aligned 06/24 and two grass strips, one 2,890 feet long (11/29)
and the other 2,200 feet long (01/19). The Garston VHF omni-directional radio
range (VOR) transmitter was installed on the south-west side of the airfield in the
mid-1960s. This is part of a radio navigation system that broadcasts a signal to
an aircraft, identifying its position. However, in the early 1970s the location was
found to be unsuitable and the apparatus was moved 5 miles away to Bovingdon,
where it is still in use today. The airfield was generally regarded to be very dry
and the drainage system excellent. The grass strips did not become boggy and
were never unserviceable. By 1989 the 01/19 grass strip had been withdrawn and
the main runway was recorded in *Pooley's Flight Guide* as being 957 metres long.
Not only did the air-traffic controllers monitor the movements of aircraft arriving
or departing Leavesden, they also provided assistance and flight information
to aircraft flying over its airspace. This service was carried out from a modern
control tower atop the administration block, completed in 1954. Due to the
proximity of the main London-to-Glasgow railway line just to the west of the
threshold of Runway 06, no take-offs or landings were permitted when a Royal
Train was about to pass; a coded message was sent to the control tower when
such an event was to occur.

While it was described as the 'Executive Terminal for London' in sales literature
in 1975, the amenities for passengers were minimal, comprising only a rest room
equipped with a drinks vending machine. This facility was, however, only a short
distance from the apron and cars could be driven up to the aircraft under the direction
of apron staff. The centre of London could be reached in under an hour via the M1
or by fast, frequent trains from Watford Junction station. Leavesden proved to be
very popular; for example in June 1965 over sixty visiting aircraft movements were
recorded, compared to fifty-odd at nearby Luton. These increased considerably over

the next few years, but a slight dip occurred in 1976 when 27,000 movements were recorded as compared to 35,000 in 1973 – a drop of 25 per cent. The lost movements were partly due to the reduction in training flights from other airfields, which used Leavesden for 'touch-and-goes' and instrument approaches. At this time the aerodrome had been running at a loss for a few years but was subsidised by Rolls-Royce. In July 1976, the Airport Consultative Committee supported Watford Borough Council's recommendation that the aerodrome continue in use as a general aviation airfield for business purposes but that there should be no intensification of use.

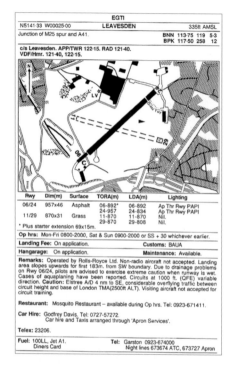

Plate from the 1989 Pooley's Flight Guide showing one asphalt and one grass runway together with other essential information for pilots. (© *Robert Pooley – reproduced with the permission of Pooley's Flight Guide*)

Above and pages 103–4: Various aerial views of the aerodrome taken in the 1970s.

Colin Morris, senior air traffic controller from 1960 to 1988, at his post in the new control tower. (*Colin Morris*)

Agusta Bell AB 204B I-AGUG and an unidentified Agusta Bell AB205 fly past the Leavesden control tower *c*. 1966. Colin Morris, senior air traffic controller, is on the left and F. C. Ridley, aerodrome manager, is on the right. (*Colin Morris*)

Beagle B 206Z XS742 of the Empire Test Pilots School at Leavesden *c.* 1966. This evaluation aircraft was the first of a batch of twenty-two Beagle B 206Zs and Basset CC-1s delivered from Shoreham between February 1965 and September 1966. First flown in January 1965, XS742 finished its days on the Boscome Down fire dump in 1968. (*Craig Woods*)

DH 104 Dove 8 G-ARHW, registered in 1961, is pictured at Leavesden in 1989. (*Grant Peerless*)

Piper PA-23 Aztec 250B G-ASHV, registered in 1963, at Leavesden. (*Richard T. Riding*)

Cessna 336 Skymaster G-ASLL, with a non-retractable undercarriage, pictured in front of the No. 1 Flight Shed at Leavesden. This aircraft was used regularly by the entertainer Hughie Green to fly Sir Billy Butlin to his holiday camps around the British Isles. Several of the Butlin camps had airstrips near them, including Bognor Regis, Pwllheli and Skegness. G-ASLL was withdrawn from use in 1974. (*Richard T. Riding*)

Beagle A-61 Terrier 2 G-ASRL – formerly WE609 and registered in 1964 – at Leavesden. It was written off in April 1969. (*Richard T. Riding*)

Beechcraft S35 Bonanza G-ATII was registered in 1965 and sold in the USA in 1981. Here it is at Leavesden in November 1970. (*Richard T. Riding*)

Alon A-2 Aircoupe G-AVIL was registered 1967 and pictured at Leavesden in November 1970, when co-author Richard Riding flew in this aircraft with Don Kendall. (*Richard T. Riding*)

Beechcraft Queen Air A-65 G-AVNA was registered in 1967 to the Guinness brewing company – note the harp logo on the fin – and is photographed here at Leavesden. It remained with this company until 1974 and transferred to the USA in 1975 as N48133. (*Richard T. Riding*)

Agusta-Bell AB-206A G-AWOY photographed at Leavesden on 3 July 1970. The helicopter was sold in Sweden in 1974. (*Richard T. Riding*)

Here photographed at Leavesden, Cessna 421B Golden Eagle G-BBSU, registered in 1973, was formerly N1509G in the USA. (*Darren J. Pitcher*)

Scottish Aviation Twin Pioneer 1 G-BCWF at Leavesden in the livery of Flight One Ltd. Originally registered G-APRS in September 1959, this Series 3 aircraft went to the Empire Test Pilots School at Farnborough in 1965 and became XT610. It was later restored to the British civil register as G-BCWF and is currently owned and operated by Air Atlantique and based at Coventry. Painted in its ETPS livery, it is the last surviving airworthy 'Twin Pin' and is affectionately known as Primrose. (*Craig Woods*)

Piper PA-28-181 Cherokee Archer II G-BRUD, formerly N8300S in the USA, was imported to the UK in 1983 and is pictured here at Leavesden in 1991. (*Craig Woods*)

The 1978 Robin R 1180T G-PACE at Leavesden. (*Darren J. Pitcher*)

Leavesden resident Rockwell Commander 114 G-TECH was originally registered in 1978 as G-BDEH. (*Darren J. Pitcher*)

De Havilland DH 104 Dove IB D-IBYC at Leavesden in July 1970. The aircraft was originally delivered to the Iraq Petroleum Company as G-AMVV in 1958 and then sold in Holland the following year. (*Richard T. Riding*)

Cessna 310P HB-LFK, once owned by Welkers Films and Crossair, photographed at Leavesden in November 1970. (*Richard T. Riding*)

Falcon Executive Aviation's Cessna 340A N3919G was built in 1977. Here it is at Leavesden on 11 August 1992. (*Grant Peerless*)

Beechcraft 65-80 Queen Air N726T photographed at Leavesden in October 1969.

Footwork's Canadair CL-600S Challenger N888FW photographed at Leavesden in 1993. (*Craig Woods*)

Beechcraft B300 King Air VR-CRI on the apron at Leavesden.

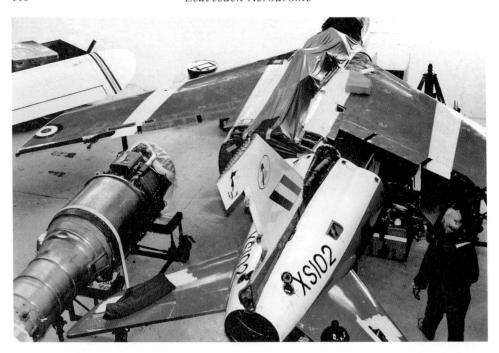

Above and below: Hawker-Siddeley Gnat XS102 seen at Leavesden during various stages of its restoration. Part of a batch of forty-one Hawker-Siddeley Gnat T-1s delivered to the RAF in 1963–64, XS102 spent its service life with 4FTS and flew as one of the RAF Yellowjacks aerobatic team, precursors of the Red Arrows. In March 1979, the aircraft was retired and was sent to RAF Halton and took up the RAF Maintenance serial number 8624M. XS102 took up civil registry as G-MOUR in 1990 and was brought up to CAA requirements by Mike Searle's company. For a time the Gnat, restored to its former Yellowjacks scheme, was owned David Gilmour of Pink Floyd. It is now operated by Delta Jets and owned by Ronan Harvey and Martin Gadsby. (*Craig Woods*)

Grumman G21A Goose N4575C receiving attention in Leavesden's Robin hangar in 1992. (*Craig Woods*)

Hunting Percival Pembroke C-1 WV740 – built nearby at Luton in 1955 – outside the old Mosquito Flight Shed at Leavesden in 1992. (*Craig Woods*)

Above and below: Consolidated PBY-5A Catalina 'JV929' G-BLSC in Dan-Air titles but still in RAF camouflage outside No. 1 Flight Shed in 1990. (*Craig Woods*).

A 1986 view inside No. 1 Flight Shed featuring, among other types, HS 125 G-HALK, Cessna 340 G-BBNR and HS 748 G-BNJK. (*Craig Woods*)

An unidentified DHC-2 Beaver of the Army Air Corps pictured at Leavesden in April 1982. (*Craig Woods*)

Fairey Swordfish LS325 was built in 1943 and spent the early part of its post-war life in civilian colours bearing the registration G-AJVH. It was presented to the RNAS at Yeovilton in 1960 and has flown in more suitable naval attire ever since. It is seen here at Leavesden in 1991. (*Craig Woods*)

A 1990 aerial view of No. 1 Flight Shed showing a variety of aircraft on the apron and grass. (*Craig Woods*)

Above and below: Short S 25 Sunderland V G-BJHS makes a pass over Leavesden. Formerly an RAF flying boat, it was sold to the Royal New Zealand Air Force in 1953. It was later converted to Sandringham configuration and flew with Ansett Flying Boat Services. The boat returned to the UK during the 1980s but in 1991 passed to Kermit Weeks's Florida-based Fantasy of Flight attraction. It is no longer airworthy. (*Craig Woods*)

Air Taxi and Charter Companies

One of the first commercial operators attracted to the facilities at Leavesden was Hunting Aerosurveys, which relocated from Elstree in 1964 and took up residence in No.1 Flight Shed. The company used a diverse variety of aircraft on survey work all over the world, including the Percival Prince, Douglas DC3, DH Dragon Rapide, DH Dove, BN Islander and Auster. Hunting Aerosurveys remained at Leavesden until 1974.

Another early commercial operator, Aircruise, moved in from Cranfield in April 1964. This company specialised in air taxi and commercial charter work using a variety of aircraft including several DH Doves and a couple of Piper Aztecs. Aircruise obtained contracts with several British companies for the provision of air charter facilities and its aircraft became familiar sights at airports both at home and abroad. One of these companies was Rolls-Royce's Aero Engine Division; Aircruise flew its executives from Leavesden to its other factories at Hucknall (Derby) and Filton (Bristol). As a result of a forced landing by a Dove in April 1965, the company's operations were scaled down, but some Cessna and Piper twins continued to be used on air-taxi work until 1969. Flight training was also undertaken using a Cessna 172. The company closed down in early 1970.

The next company to take up residence was Eagle Aircraft Services, part of the Bamberg Group of companies, which moved in from Gatwick on 1 April 1967. Eagle was to remain at Leavesden until it ceased operations in February 1984. The company held the British franchise for the full range of Beech aircraft and as well as the sale of new and used models it also offered a complete maintenance service. By 1981, the company employed 170 personnel at Leavesden and other sites in the UK. In addition, the company undertook air-taxi and charter work with its Air Operator's Certificate, using mostly Beech King Airs, Queen Airs and Barons, some from its own stock of new and used aircraft. Other companies operated under Eagle's certificate, including Baron Air Charter of Southend, which flew the first Beech 58 Baron imported into this country.

Webster Aviation was founded in 1969 and specialised mainly in the sale of executive twin aircraft, based in Flight Shed No. 2. It had an associated company, Ambrion Aviation, which was a Cessna dealer and supplied Piper spares. The company was dissolved in 1981.

In June 1972, Directair was formed at Leavesden as another air taxi/executive charter company and by August that year it was operating a Piper Aztec, Twin Comanche and Navajo. Directair subsequently acquired Southend Air Taxis in November 1973 and as a result three further Piper twins were added to the fleet. The company took over the Southend base and also opened up at Aberdeen and Norwich for operations on lucrative oil exploration flights. However, Directair experienced financial difficulties and several aircraft were impounded in December 1974. All flying had ceased by the following January.

The next company to set up at Leavesden was Speedwell Air Charter in the spring of 1974, but it only operated for just over two years, ceasing all flying in October 1976. In its short life, it used a single Piper Aztec on air-taxi flights and also leased this aircraft to other operators.

Alvis Leonides-powered Percival P-50 Prince 3E G-AMLZ, registered 1951 and withdrawn from use in 1971, is seen here at Leavesden in July 1970. (*Richard T. Riding*)

DH 104 Dove 8 G-ARHX, belonging to Hunting Surveys Ltd, was withdrawn from use in 1978. It is seen here in front of the No. 1 Flight Shed at Leavesden. (*Richard T. Riding*)

Above and below: Two photographs of BN-2A Islander G-AWNT, built and registered in 1968. It is seen here at Leavesden in two different liveries: Hunting Aerofilms and Aerofilms. (*Craig Woods*)

Reims Cessna 172G G-ATKU was registered in 1965 and operated by Aircruise from Leavesden. (*Richard T. Riding*)

Fairweather's Cessna 337B Super Skymaster G-AVIX (with retractable undercarriage) was registered in 1967 and operated by Aircruise. It is seen here at Leavesden and was re-registered G-RORO in 1980. (*Richard T. Riding*)

Beechcraft E95 Travel Air G-AWCW was registered to Eagle Aircraft Services in 1968; here it

Beechcraft A23-19A Musketeer G-AWTV registered in 1968 to Eagle Aircraft Services. Here it is photographed at Leavesden in October 1969. (*Richard T. Riding*)

DH 104 Dove 5 G-AROI *Eaglet,* seen at Leavesden in British Eagle livery. It later passed to Fairflight and was based at Biggin Hill. (*Richard T. Riding*)

Piper Twin Comanche 160 G-ASSR, registered in 1964 to Direct Air Ltd, is here photographed at Leavesden in July 1970. (*Richard T. Riding*)

Yet another air taxi/executive charter company was established at Leavesden in the shape of Executive Express in early 1975, equipped with the ubiquitous Piper Navajo. It operated two examples of this type on flights all over Britain and the Continent until it was dissolved in December 1987.

A company advertising its services in *Flight International* in September 1975 was Hiller Aviation, which specialised in the sale of Hiller 12E helicopters for use in police patrol, aerial survey, forestry, crop spraying and training. This company was relatively short-lived, having been set up around 1974 and wound up five years later in 1979.

Leavesden Air Servicing was set up in August 1963 and offered a comprehensive service to general aviation, including Certificate of Airworthiness renewals, avionics overhaul, structural repairs and modifications, and engineering support for overseas operations. The company was wound up in September 1988.

Scheduled Services

A significant development took place in 1970 when scheduled services were introduced from Leavesden by Humber Airways. A combination of traffic density and high handling charges at Heathrow led to Humber's choice of Leavesden, the idea being to connect with fast trains to Euston from Watford Junction station. However, this venture was initially beset with problems as Eagle Flying Services, also based at Leavesden, objected to Humber's application to the Air Transport Licensing Board. The grounds were (1) that Eagle wished to open up a network of routes that included some of those proposed by Humber, (2) Leavesden was not a suitable airfield for passenger services, and (3) the Islander aircraft proposed was unsuitable when compared with the Beech 99, which Eagle had in mind. Luckily Eagle withdrew its objections and Humber was granted a licence to operate a route to Hull, the inaugural flight taking place on 16 March 1970. Two Britten-Norman Islander aircraft were used for the operation, namely *Apollo* and *Juno*, which kept alive the names of two former ships of Humber's parent company, Ellerman's Wilson Line.

The service was not exactly popular, possibly due to the strange choice of destination; in the first week only fifty-seven passengers were carried, but by the end of May the figure had reached 1,000. Two morning flights and one evening flight from Hull to Leavesden were flown, and in the other direction one morning flight and two evening ones. This emphasised the fact that Humber was catering more for the Hull-based businessman than his London-based counterpart. Flight time was sixty-five minutes and the return fare was £14.70 (about £170 today – not exactly a low-cost carrier). This compared with the first-class rail fare of £9 (about £100 today). Facilities at Leavesden were not particularly luxurious – the passenger lounge was a basic but functional hut and Board of Trade regulations stated that each passenger had to be weighed before boarding. Humber tactfully put the bathroom scales used for this purpose in an adjoining room. Initially the former Blackburn Aircraft Company airfield at Brough was used as the Hull terminal, but the construction of a very tall chimney on the approach to the runway precluded further air-transport operations. A new home had to be found and on 23 November 1970 the RAF airfield at Leconfield became the new terminal. By this time, 3,500 passengers had been carried along the route. Flushed with success, Humber commenced a new service to the Hawker Siddeley airfield at Chester (Hawarden) on 5 October 1970 – again an odd choice, but one previously considered by Eagle. Unfortunately these two routes were not a financial success (to break even they needed seven passengers per flight, but only managed to average four) and they were suspended on 30 September 1971 after eighteen months on the Hull run and only three months to Chester. Following the demise of Humber Airways, no more scheduled services were operated to or from Leavesden.

Airship Operations

During June 1973, a series of promotional flights were made from Leavesden by the Goodyear airship *Europa* as part of a European tour. Co-author Richard Riding was one of the lucky passengers on two of these flights and was accompanied on one of them by John Houlder, the manager of Elstree Aerodrome. *Europa*, the 300th airship built by Goodyear, was assembled not far from Leavesden, at Cardington in Bedfordshire, at a cost of £1.25 million (about £11.3 million today). She was powered by two 210 hp engines and cruised at around 1,000 feet at a speed of 35–40 mph, carrying six passengers. *Europa* could often be seen over major sporting events such as motor and yacht races as she provided a stable camera platform for filming. She was also equipped with over 7,500 coloured light bulbs for night-time advertising and displaying messages.

A programme of pleasure flights over London's scenic landmarks in a Skyship 500 took place from 23 April to 28 June 1986. It was claimed that these were the first fare-paying passenger flights in an airship for nearly fifty years, i.e. since the *Hindenburg* disaster of 1937. Four passengers paid £100 each (about £220 today) for the flights, which lasted just under an hour. British Caledonian Airways initially sponsored the operation to the tune of £150,000 (about £330,000 today) and in return the company's logo was emblazoned on the Skyship. Michael Spicer, the Aviation Minister, was a passenger on the inaugural flight and he was joined by the managing director and technical director of Airship Industries (the manufacturer of the Skyship) and Sir Peter Masefield, the well-known aviator. Unfortunately this first flight did not reach London because of adverse weather conditions, but it was nevertheless enjoyed by all on board. An added attraction for passengers was the opportunity to view at close quarters the *EastEnders* set at nearby Elstree Studios.

However, not everybody was happy as forty-five complaints were made to Watford Borough Council about noise and invasion of privacy due to the low altitude of the flights. Despite these complaints, the operation's popularity was not diminished as there were still 3,500 people on the waiting list when the flights ceased from Leavesden.

TIME TABLE
1 MAY
TO
30 SEPTEMBER 1971

HULL
LONDON
HULL

| Booking Offices | LEAVESDEN Garston (Herts.) 76580/89 (no S.T.D. Code) |
| | LECONFIELD 04015-625/7 (after hours Hull 0482 652546) |

 **HUMBER AIRWAYS LIMITED**

Make time

...fly!

BY **HAL**

Brough to central London in under 2 hours — how's that for making time?

Brough-Leavesden	Departs	Arrives
Flight No. H M 101	0745	0850
Flight No. H M 103	0815	0920
Flight No. H M 105	1715	1820

Leavesden - Brough	Departs	Arrives
Flight No. H M 102	0905	1010
Flight No. H M 104	1730	1835
Flight No. H M 106	1835	1940

MONDAY TO FRIDAY INCLUSIVE

Fast Road & Rail Services from Watford to Euston, Heathrow etc.
SERVICES COMMENCE MARCH 16TH
Book at Brough Airport or through your Travel Agent

Your Local Airline
HUMBER AIRWAYS LTD
BROUGH AIRPORT · BROUGH · Tel: Hull 667168/9
After Hours Telephone: Hull 668326 or Keyingham 2363

HUMBER AIRWAYS

WINTER
TIMETABLE

5th October 1970—31st March 1971

The information contained in this timetable is based on the latest information available at the time of going to press and is subject to alteration without notice.
CONDITIONS OF CARRIAGE
The carriage of passengers, baggage and cargo is subject to Humber Airways General Conditions of Carriage and Regulations, which may be seen on request at any Humber Airways Booking Office.

HULL—LONDON
CHESTER—LONDON

This page and opposite, above: Timetables and schedules for Humber Airways' services from Leavesden in 1970/71. (*The Michael Dawes Collection*)

HULL—LONDON	Mon.–Fri.	
Flight No.	HM 101	HM 105
Dep. Leconfield	0820	1700
Arr. Leavesden	0930	1810
Dep. Leavesden	0935	1815
Dep. Watford	0954	1828
Arr. London (Euston)	1014	1847

LONDON—HULL	Mon.–Fri.	
Flight No.	HM 102	HM 106
Dep. London (Euston)	0835	1730
Arr. Watford	0855	1748
Dep. Watford	0900	1753
Dep. Leavesden	0940	1820
Arr. Leconfield	1050	1930

Final check-in 10 mins. before departure

FARES	SINGLE	RETURN
Air	£8·10	£16·20
Coach (Watford) (Leavesden)	12½p	25p
Excess Baggage	10p per Kilo	
Cargo Rates	Minimum £1·00	
Up to 45 Kg.	10p per Kilo	
Over 45 Kg.	8p per Kilo	

CHILDREN—AIR FARES
Under 2 years free
2 years and under 12 years half the adult Fare

AIRPORTS

HULL—
CIVIL AIR TERMINAL R.A.F. LECONFIELD
LONDON—
ROLLS-ROYCE AIRFIELD, LEAVESDEN
(Intersection of A41 and A405)
Car Parks are available at the Airports

Car Hire and Transport Facilities. Arrangements for hire of cars, taxis etc., can be made at any Humber Airways Office.
There is a mini bus which serves the flights at Leavesden Airport. Details of timings are shown in the timetable.
A fast and frequent Electric Train Service operates between Watford Junction and Euston which takes about 20 minutes.
Current timings of all these services can be obtained from Humber Airways Limited but it is stressed that Humber Airways Limited have no connection whatsoever with these services and give details merely for guidance.

INTERLINE Connections
Humber Airways can arrange transport by executive car to all Airports. Approximate journey time to Heathrow Airport 45 minutes—charge £3 (Approx.)
A Green Line Coach Service operates between Watford Junction and Heathrow Airport and direct connections with Luton and Gatwick are also available.

EXECUTIVE AIR CHARTER
AIR TAXI—THE MANAGEMENT TOOL THAT SAVES TIME—AND CAN SAVE MONEY
HUMBER AIRWAYS HAVE TWO—THE ISLANDER (9 SEATS) AND A PIPER AZTEC (5 SEATS)

ANYWHERE — ANYTIME

TRANSPORT
Transport between the Airport and City centres is the responsibility of the passenger. The following information is given only for guidance and Humber Airways Ltd. cannot be held responsible for any omissions or errors.

HULL. Frequent passenger train service between Brough and Hull.

LONDON. Humber Airways provide Coach link between Leavesden and Watford Junction —Fare 2/6 single. Coaches depart Watford Junction at 0840, 1710 and 1810 for Leavesden.

Fast Train service between Watford Junction and Euston.

HEATHROW/LUTON. Green 727 Bus Service operates from Watford Junction.

BOOKING OFFICES:

Leavesden
ROLLS ROYCE AIRFIELD
Telephone: Garston 76580/76589

Brough
BROUGH AIRPORT
Telephone: Brough 667168/667169

BN-2A6 Islander G-AXRM *Apollo*, built in 1968 and registered to Humber Airways in 1969, was sold to the USA in 1975 and became N158MA. It is photographed at Leavesden. (*Richard T. Riding*)

Below and pages 133–5: This series of photographs of the Goodyear Airship N2A were taken at Leavesden in June 1973. Co-author Richard Riding had two flights in the airship, on 22 and 31 June. The pilot was A. Brizon and each flight lasted forty minutes and consisted of cruising around the local area at 35 knots at 1,500 feet.

In 1968 the Goodyear Tire & Rubber Company announced a major expansion programme, which led to the construction of four non-rigid GZ-20-type airships: *Mayflower*, *Columbia*, *America* and *Europa*. *Europa*, the 300th airship to be built by Goodyear since 1917, was to be based at Capena near Rome and cover major events for film and broadcasting companies. The components for *Europa* were made at Goodyear's Akron factory in Ohio and flown over by Guppy to England and assembled at Cardington early 1972. The airship's first flight was made on 8 March, but disaster struck when, on 19 March, the airship was wrenched from its moorings and ended up in a tree. Repair work was carried out and another envelope was supplied by the Akron facility. After repair *Europa* was flown from Cardington on 25 June in time to cover the ill-fated Munich Olympic Games.

With a surface area of 21,600 square feet, *Europa's* envelope was made of two-ply Neoprene-coated Dacron, which held 202,700 cubic feet of non-flammable helium. The airship was powered by two 210 hp Continental six-cylinder horizontally-opposed air cooled engines, one on either side of the gondola, driving two twin-blade reversible-pitch pusher propellers. The gondola accommodated six passengers and two crew. It was equipped with a total of 7,560 miniature light bulbs for nocturnal messages, but not advertising. An external APU, mounted on the underside of the gondola, provided a generator to power the lights. *Europa* was 192 feet long and had a diameter of 46 feet. In still air, the maximum speed was 50 mph. Endurance with auxiliary tanks was twenty-three hours. Her gross weight was 12,840 lb and empty she weighed 9,375 lb. *Europa* had an impressive climb rate of 2,400 feet per minute – nerve-racking to a fixed-wing pilot. One must also remember that airships go up when the sun comes out.

By 1975, *Europa* had carried 20,000 passengers and flown around 4,000 hours. During the ensuing years she carried out aerial TV coverage of many major UK events until chartered by the BBC for wildlife filming in the Carmague region of France. During this period the airship was destroyed when it was dashed to the ground in a severe down draught in torrential rain. The envelope was repaired *in situ* and returned with the gondola to Goodyear at Akron and stored. Years later, in 1998, the gondola was attached to a new airship, *Stars and Stripes*.

The ground handlers hold down *Europa* as she prepares for take-off. The lettering and logo were blue and the ship was silver. (*Richard T. Riding*)

Nearly ready to cast off. (*Richard T. Riding*)

Europa N2A passes over Leavesden on another sightseeing flight in June 1973. (*Richard T. Riding*)

A photograph difficult to resist taking when one is up there, chased by a shadow of the past – in this case over Watford. (*Richard T. Riding*)

Coming in to land at Leavesden, with the mobile mooring mast just visible in front of the second pilot's nose. (*Richard T. Riding*)

The ground handlers move forward to grab hold of the mooring ropes and to add ballast as the passengers make their exit. (*Richard T. Riding*)

A final look at *Europa* as she prepares for another flight. (*Richard T. Riding*)

Skyship 500 G-BIHN at Leavesden in the spring of 1986 when it was used for a series of pleasure flights. This non-rigid airship was famously featured in *A View to Kill*, the James Bond film in which it is flown by the villain Max Zorin. Slightly larger than Goodyear's *Europa*, G-BIHN was 216 feet 5 inches long and carried twelve passengers and two crew. It even had a lavatory on board. It cruised at 40 mph and had a still-air maximum speed of 65 mph. It was powered by two 255 hp Porsche 930 engines. (*Watford Observer*)

Flying Training

Flying training was always popular at Leavesden and many organisations came and went over the years. These included Leavesden Flying School (which was set up in around 1968 but moved to Panshanger in November 1969) and David Fairclough & Co. trading as DF Aviation, which commenced operations in August 1975 before also moving to Panshanger in 1980. Leavesden Flight Centre was formed in 1985 and became Bonus Aviation. When Leavesden closed in March 1994, the company moved to Cranfield, where it still operates today.

In 1986, Fowler Aviation was offering training courses for the Private Pilot's Licence. Donoghue Aviation operated in the training role briefly between 1987 and 1990, but in June of that month its aircraft were reclaimed and at least forty-two student pilots were left out of pocket. Flyteam Aviation was established in June 1990 and specialised in self-fly hire, moving to Cranfield and Elstree on the demise of Leavesden. The Panshanger School of Flying transferred to Leavesden after Panshanger closed temporarily in April 1992, but had to relocate again to a private strip at High Cross near Ware when Leavesden closed. Firecrest Aviation, another training school, moved to Elstree after Leavesden's demise; it is still going strong. Although not based at Leavesden, Executive Flying Club

The Leavesden Flight Centre logo.

Leavesden Flight Centre's Piper PA-38 Tomahawk G-OLFC photographed in 1989. In June 2007, the aircraft suffered an accident at a private strip in Cheshire and was later converted into a flight simulator and based at Hesket Market. (*Grant Peerless*)

used the aerodrome for training between 1977 and 1980, since its home base at Panshanger was not licensed at that time. Resident private flying groups included MKM Flying Group, Colt Flying Group, Uniform Oscar Group, Croxley Flying Group and Aiglet Flying Group.

Leavesden was also the base for a large number of company and privately owned aircraft from business jets to single-engined trainers and helicopters. Just prior to its closure, nearly ninety were resident.

Jetstream Refurbishment

Following the demise of Handley Page Aircraft Ltd in March 1970, Capt. W. J. (Bill) Bright of Terravia Trading Services Ltd purchased the stocks of Jetstream aircraft together with design drawings, documentation, inspection records, CAA records, spares and ground equipment for a reported £250,000 (about £2.9 million today). Between August and October 1970, twenty-one Jetstreams were moved from Radlett to Sywell, Northamptonshire, and a new company, Jetstream Aircraft Ltd, was set up. The Sywell base was short-lived and operations were transferred to Flight Shed No. 2 at Leavesden in June 1971. Here the company refurbished five of the Jetstreams, which included painting, fitting out interiors, the installation of avionics, and test-flying. The last aircraft was delivered in January 1975. Unfortunately this operation did not find favour with local residents, who objected to the test flying in particular and the expansion of the aerodrome in general.

AA-1 Yankee franchise

A short-lived operation was set up at Leavesden in July 1971 by General Aviation Sales of Jersey to distribute the American Aviation AA-1 Yankee. Half a dozen or so were imported from the USA and some of these were sold in Norway, but the firm ceased to exist a couple of years later. However, the AA-1 evolved into the AA-5 Cheetah/AG-5 Tiger series and became extremely popular with flying schools and private owners.

St John Ambulance Air Wing

This was formed in 1972 by Peter Leuchars, commissioner-in-chief of St John Ambulance, to provide the rapid transport of patients in need of specialist attention as well as organs, drugs and blood supplies. It was based at St Margaret's Hospital, Epping. Many of these mercy flights used Leavesden and pilots worked on a voluntary basis, flying their company aircraft. They received only out-of-pocket expenses. Sadly the wing was disbanded in 1993, due to economic pressures; chartered aircraft were then used.

Piper PA-38 112 Tomahawk G-BNPM, formerly N2561D in the USA, was first registered in 1989 and was operated by the Leavesden Flight Centre. (*Craig Woods*)

Piper PA-22-108 Colt G-ARNJ at Leavesden on 29 April 1989. This aircraft was owned by the MKM Flying Group from May 1977 to February 1989. One of the 'Ms' in MKM was Colin Morris, who was an air traffic controller at the aerodrome at the time. It is still on the civil register today, based in the Liverpool area. (*Derek Heley*)

Handley Page 137 Jetstream 200 G-BBYM, registered in 1974 to the Morgan Crucible Company, was one of a batch of Jetstreams refurbished at Leavesden in the early 1970s. It was registered G-AYWR prior to refurbishment. (*David Johnstone*)

A view of American Aviation AA-1 Yankee G-AYLP, pictured outside the old Mosquito flight shed in March 1971. (*Richard T. Riding*)

American Aviation AA-5B Yankee LN-KAJ, pictured at Leavesden in November 1970, later became OY-AYA. (*Richard T. Riding*)

American Aviation AA-5 Yankee LN-KAZ photographed at Leavesden in November 1970. (*Richard T. Riding*)

A line-up of newly imported American Aviation AA-1 Yankees at Leavesden in March 1971. They were all registered in October 1970 and are seen here shortly after assembly. G-AYLN, nearest the camera, was written off in 1978, G-AYLO was damaged beyond repair in September 1984, G-AYLP was sold in Ireland in August 1972 as EI-AVV but returned to the UK in 2003 and is now based at Henstridge, and G-AYLM was re-registered G-SEXY in June 1981 and is now displayed by Speke Aerodrome Heritage Group in the Crowne Plaza, Liverpool. The two virginal Yankees in the background may have been those that were exported to Norway. Co-author Richard Riding flew in G-AYLO and G-AYLP in March 1971 to take publicity photographs for the importers of the aircraft. (*Richard T. Riding*)

CHAPTER FIVE

OTHER ACTIVITIES

The skills, adaptability and enthusiasm of the Leavesden workforce built up over many years ensured that it stayed competitive. The manufacture of DH and, later, Rolls-Royce products required the use of the latest state-of-the-art techniques, together with the best use of traditional methods. Other activities included the following:

Nuclear Power

In 1954, the DH Engine Company developed an interest in nuclear power and specialist staff were attached to the Atomic Energy Research Establishment at Harwell to look into the possibility of using this form of energy for propulsion purposes. A major part of this task concerned investigation into high-temperature, gas-cooled reactors (HTGCR) and DH set up a specialist team, the Nuclear Power Group, to carry out research into HTGCRs. This side of the DH operation was eventually wound up following its incorporation into Bristol Siddeley.

Welding

In the early 1950s, the DH Engine Company's welding engineers worked closely with the British Oxygen Company to develop argon-welding techniques for the then-new stainless steel and nimonic alloys being used in the manufacture of jet engines. They also diversified into the manufacture of part of the Sultzer turbo blower for railway locomotives, turbo drills for oil rigs, and garage forecourt dispensing equipment.

Motorcycle Engines

In 1952 the DH Engine Company, in conjunction with the Vincent Company, developed a two-stroke motorcycle engine based on the Gipsy. A further collaboration with Austrian motorcycle enthusiast Dr Joseph Ehrlich's company EMC produced a 125 cc engine, which achieved considerable success in the late 1950s/early 1960s in the hands of some of the foremost riders of the time, including Mike Hailwood, Rex Avery and Derek Minter.

Marine Engines

Another departure for the DH Engine Company in the early 1960s, again in collaboration with Ehrlich, was the experimental 'Water Gipsy' two-stroke outboard motor of 10 hp/150 cc. It was aimed at the expanding boating leisure market but did not go into production.

In 1947, Sir Malcolm Campbell carried out trials with a Goblin jet engine in his *Bluebird K4* speedboat, but these were unsuccessful. Later, a Ghost engine powered John Cobb's speedboat *Crusader*, which broke up on Loch Ness while trying to beat the world waterspeed record on 29 September 1952. Sadly, Cobb was killed in the attempt.

Farming

During the 1950s and early 1960s, DH operated a profitable farm on its Leavesden site and won several awards for its livestock.

CHAPTER SIX

EVENTS AND PERSONALITIES

Films

A foretaste of things to come, the following is a selection of films and TV series made at Leavesden before the aerodrome closed:

- 1959: Scenes filmed for ITV's *The Invisible Man* (series 2, episode 1, 'Point of Destruction'). Saboteurs loose in London cause four fatal air accidents. Dr Peter Brady arrives at the aerodrome to investigate the crashes. Screened 12 April 1959.
- 13 March 1974: Opening sequence of episode 175 of the BBC's *This Is Your Life* featuring Sheila Scott, the well-known aviatrix, filmed in a Leavesden flight hangar. Sheila Scott was a regular user of the aerodrome.
- October 1976: Filming of TV commercial for Datsun cars featuring the actor Jack Hedley.
- July 1977: Scenes filmed for an episode of ITV's *The Professionals* (series 1, episode 6, 'Where the Jungle Ends'). A group of mercenaries dressed as soldiers rob a bank and escape in a Cessna 421 aircraft from the aerodrome. Screened 3 February 1978.
- 24 June 1986: Part of Channel 4's *Treasure Hunt* (series 5, episode 6) filmed on the aerodrome. Royal Navy Sea Harrier formated with Anneka Rice's Jet Ranger helicopter and both landed. Pilot of the Harrier had the clue. Screened on 19 March 1987.

Personalities

Leavesden was honoured with visits by a variety of personalities, including:

- 1970: New clubhouse for the Sports and Social Club opened by the comedian Dick Emery.
- 10 October 1974: Visit by HRH The Duke of Kent to Rolls-Royce Small Engines Division.
- 1960s/1970s: Visit by Sir Harry Secombe.
- Late 1970s: The singer Roger Whittaker gained his Private Pilot's Licence at Leavesden and went on to own, among several other aeroplanes, the appropriately registered Beech Super King Air G-SONG and Beech Duke G-SING.

TV personality Anneka Rice sitting in Bell Jet Ranger G-BHXU after landing at Leavesden on 24 June 1986 as part of Channel 4's *Treasure Hunt* programme. The helicopter had just formated with Royal Navy Sea Harrier ZD581 of 899 Squadron over the airfield. Both aircraft landed and the pilot of the Harrier handed over the clue. (*Watford Observer*)

- April 1978: BBC *Nationwide* presenter Barry Bowles reached over 200 mph in six seconds along Leavesden's runway in the rocket-propelled car *Blonde Bombshell*.
- November 1976/78: Visit by the astronaut John Glenn.
- 1989: Sir Frank Whittle, father of the jet engine, visits the Rolls-Royce Small Engines Division.
- 30 October 1965: Not a human personality, but the famous DH Comet Racer G-ACSS *Grosvenor House*, which had been stored at Leavesden since being exhibited at the Festival of Britain in 1951, was moved to the Shuttleworth Collection at Old Warden, Bedfordshire.

Ghosts

The ghost of an RAF corporal is said to haunt the area. One night in 1941 when the aerodrome was being battered by gale-force winds, the corporal attempted to open the doors of No. 2 Hangar. The door was operated by a chain attached to a ratchet and as he tried to open it an especially strong gust of wind blew the door down on top of him and he was killed. Afterwards, on windy nights, the chains were said to rattle even though the hangar was long gone.

HRH The Duke of Kent visits Leavesden on 10 October 1974. He had just arrived in a Wessex helicopter of the Queen's Flight, which was appropriately powered by Rolls-Royce Gnome engines built at Leavesden. (*Craig Woods*)

Sir Frank Whittle, second from right, visits the Rolls-Royce Small Engine Division at Leavesden in 1989.

Flying Displays

Open days were a popular feature at Leavesden from 1947 until 1988. They included flying displays, tours of the factories, sports activities and attractions for families. At one such event in June 1953, lucky programme holders enjoyed free flights in a DH Dove and Sir Geoffrey and Lady de Havilland arrived in a DH Heron from Hatfield. The 1972 open day celebrated Watford Borough's Golden Jubilee, while the 1980 event featured the Red Arrows and the Battle of Britain Memorial Flight among a varied programme. The highlight of the 1987 open day was a display by a British Airways Concorde. Another Concorde belonging to Air France took part in the last open day in 1988, and this event attracted more than 35,000 visitors in 10,000 cars. Both Concordes carried lucky Rolls-Royce employees and their families on chartered supersonic flights. Concorde was not able to land or take off from Leavesden's relatively short runway, but still provided spectacular low-level displays. There should have been one last open day in 1990, but this was cancelled at the last minute due to industrial action by Rolls-Royce employees, who pledged to stage mass demonstrations at the event.

A poster for 1978 Vintage Air Display at Leavesden. (*RAF Museum*)

The covers of the open-day programmes from 1974, 1980, 1984 and 1987.

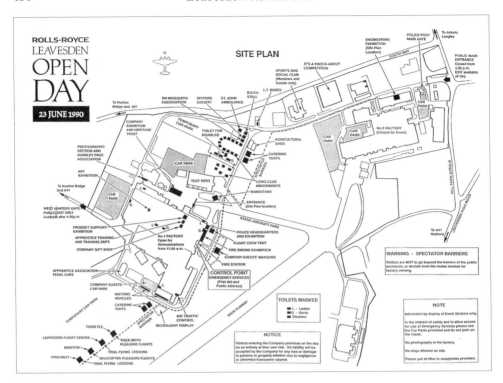

The site plan in the programme for the ill-fated open day that should have taken place in 1990 but was cancelled at the last moment due to threatened industrial action by Rolls-Royce employees.

A DH 114 Heron crosses Leavesden during the 7 July 1951 open day. (*Watford Observer*)

Looking across the signals square at the de Havilland Engine Company's Percival Proctor I G-AHMP at the 1951 open day. The Proctor was withdrawn from use in 1963. (*BAE Systems*)

Aerial view of the 1951 open day at Leavesden taken from the de Havilland Engine Company's Percival Proctor 1 G-AHMP. Parked on the grass are a DH98 Mosquito, DH103 Hornet, DH104 Dove, DHC1 Chipmunk and possibly a Vampire. (*Watford Observer*)

Three aerial views of Leavesden during an open day in the 1950s.

DH 51 G-EBIR, owned by the Shuttleworth Collection, at an open day at Leavesden on 30 June 1973. Built in 1928 and delivered to Kenya as VP-KAA, the aircraft was returned to the UK in 1972 and restored to the British register. It still makes the occasional flight from its Old Warden base. (*Mike Hooks*)

Masquerading as a Messerschmitt Bf 109, G-ASTG is a Nord 1002 Pingouin, formerly F-BGKI from France. It is seen here at Leavesden on the 30 June 1973 open day. The aircraft was withdrawn from use shortly after this photograph was taken. (*Mike Hooks*)

This North American Harvard IIB (AT-16) formerly flew in Holland as PH-SKK. For several years it was painted white and owned by rock musician Gary Numan, who flew it with another Harvard to form the Radial Pair aerobatic duo. It is currently owned by the Goodwood Aero Club. Here it is seen with its British civil registration G-AZSC at the Leavesden open day of 30 June 1973. (*Mike Hooks*)

1945 Supermarine Spitfire LFXVIe SL721/G-BAUP in the colours of the aircraft flown by ACM Sir James Robb; he used it as his personal hack in the RAF from 1946. At the time this photograph was taken at a Leavesden open day, the Spitfire was owned by Doug Arnold. Since then, the aircraft has spent two spells in the USA and is currently owned by Vintage Wings in Canada, where it is registered C-CVZB. Note the Goodyear airship *Europa* in the background. (*Mike Hooks*)

CCF AT-6 Harvard 4 FT339 at Leavesden at the 30 June 1973 open day. Built by the Canadian Car Foundry, the aircraft was registered G-BIWX. (*Mike Hooks*)

Pitts 2-AE Special G-PITS at the 1987 Leavesden open day. (*Grant Peerless*)

Tiger Club member Lewis Benjamin flying the club's DH82A single-seat Tiger Moth G-ANMZ with Lollie as wing-walker at a Battle of Britain display at Leavesden on 19 September 1964. This aircraft served with the Tiger Club for nearly twenty years until it was destroyed in May 1981. (*Lewis Benjamin*)

Westland Sea King Mk 48 RS02 of 40 Squadron 19 Wing – usually kept at the Koksijde Air Base of the Belgian Air Force – at the 1986 open day. (*Craig Woods*)

Air France Concorde F-BVFF performing a flypast at the 1988 open day. (*Craig Woods*)

Another view of Air France Concorde F-BVFF over the Leavesden control tower at the 1988 open day. (*Craig Woods*)

DHC-1 Chipmunk Mk 22 G-BBMT, formerly WP831 with the RAF, at an open day in the 1980s. (*Craig Woods*)

A major event in July 1953 was the Queen's Coronation Review of the RAF. The airspace over Leavesden Aerodrome was the official joining-up point for 643 aircraft of twenty-six widely varying types from forty-three airfields throughout Britain. They flew in a continuous stream to RAF Odiham in Hampshire, where the review took place. The parade was led by Flt Lt Danny Kearns in a Bristol Sycamore helicopter. In later years, Danny was to become Leavesden's customer relations manager.

The Amelia Earhart Air Race to Londonderry, Northern Ireland, started from Leavesden on several occasions in the 1980s. Supported by the Royal Aero Club, this event qualified pilots for the King's Cup race.

To celebrate the Queen Mother's ninetieth birthday on 4 August 1990, some fourteen Westland Lynx and Sea King helicopters formed up at Leavesden for a fly-past over Central London.

The aerodrome was used regularly for overnight hangarage of Spitfires and Hurricanes belonging to the RAF's Battle of Britain Memorial Flight in order to position them for flying displays in the south of the country. They inevitably 'beat up' Leavesden on their return, which provided a thrilling spectacle for local residents.

The Social Side

From humble beginnings in the early 1950s, the Sports and Social Club operated from a small converted wartime building. The vision and hard work of its members over the following years, together with company help, enabled a modern clubhouse to be built; it was opened in 1970 by the comedian Dick Emery. The new club building comprised comfortable lounges, a fully air-conditioned ballroom, games rooms, changing rooms, a snack bar and a TV lounge – all of which made it the most up-to-date club house for miles around.

The Royal Air Forces Association

Rolls-Royce Leavesden was unique in having its own branch (1260) of the Royal Air Forces Association (RAFA); it was one of very few such branches in the country.

Various aircraft assembled at Leavesden for the start of the 1983 Amelia Earhart Air Race to Londonderry, Northern Ireland. (*Geoff Whitmore*)

Probably the most famous Hawker Hurricane of them all is PZ865, *The Last of the Many*, a Mk 2c built in 1944 and for a while registered G-AMAU. Originally owned by Hawker Aircraft Ltd, the Hurricane was presented to the Battle of Britain Memorial Flight (BBMF) by Hawker Siddeley in March 1972. In this 1990 shot taken at Leavesden, Cessna F 182Q G-BGOH can be see landing in the background. (*Craig Woods*)

Supermarine Spitfire PR XIX PS853, here pictured at Leavesden in 1992, was built in 1944 and delivered to the RAF in 1945. In 1957 it was issued to the newly formed Battle of Britain Memorial Flight at Biggin Hill. The aircraft was acquired by Rolls-Royce in 1997. (*Craig Woods*)

Battle of Britain Memorial Flight's Supermarine Spitfire PR XIX PM631 at Leavesden in 1990. Built in 1945, this Spitfire retired from RAF service in 1957 and was issued to the newly formed BBMF at Biggin Hill. It is seen here painted to represent an aircraft of 11 Squadron and bears the name *Mary* on its nose. PM631 is the BBMF's longest serving aircraft. The BBMF's Hurricanes and Spitfires were regularly positioned at Leavesden in the summer months. (*Craig Woods*)

CHAPTER SEVEN

CRASHES AND OTHER INCIDENTS

Although a busy aerodrome, Leavesden mercifully witnessed few major accidents during its fifty-four years of operation. There were, however, a number of incidents and the following is a selection:

21 January 1934 – de Havilland DH60 Moth

This Moth belonging to the London Aeroplane Club crash-landed near the junction of High Road and Russell Lane, close to the site of the future Leavesden Aerodrome. The pilot was Scott McMurdo and his wife was the passenger. Scott suffered a broken nose and Mrs McMurdo received a leg injury.

23 November 1942 – Boeing B-17F 41-24506 'DF-G' *The Shiftless Skonk*

Belonging to 324th Bomb Squadron, 91st Bomb Group USAAF, *The Shiftless Skonk* was on its final approach for an emergency landing after being badly damaged when it hit an electricity pylon and crashed near the Black Boy public house, Bricket Wood, 2 miles short of the runway. Five crew members were killed and five survived.

1944 – Airspeed Horsa

This glider became detached from its towing aircraft and landed on the aerodrome. It still had its tow line attached, which knocked some roof tiles from a house in High Road.

26 September 1944 – Mosquito NF30 MT480

This Mosquito crashed on returning from a test flight. Pilot Sqn Ldr Cox was unhurt.

31 October 1945 – North American Texan 44-81719

The aircraft's port undercarriage leg collapsed on landing.

20 December 1951 – De Havilland Mosquito NF36 RK998

On a flight from Coltishall, Capt. Gatterfield mistook Leavesden for Hatfield and overshot the runway after landing.

A poor newsprint photograph of an unidentified DH 60 Moth that crashed at Leavesden on 22 January 1934, injuring Mrs Scott McMurdo, a dancer. Her husband was the pilot and he escaped with just a broken nose.

16 December 1957 – De Havilland Dove 6 OE-FAC

This brand new aircraft (the 500th Dove built) arrived from Hatfield for fitting out but undershot the landing and was damaged beyond repair.

15 December 1965 – Beagle A109 Airedale G-ASWB

The engine of this machine, which was owned by Kebbell Developments & United Marine Ltd, cut on landing and the aircraft was damaged.

20 October 1971 – Beechcraft 35-C33 Debonair G-AVHG

This aircraft, owned by GD & HM Colover and Bingham Plastics Ltd, landed with its undercarriage retracted.

13 July 1976 – Cessna F150H G-AVUH

This aircraft, belonging to the Luton Flying Club, bounced on landing. The nose wheel collapsed.

27 January 1979 – Rockwell Commander 685 N135EX

A friend of the pilot walked into a moving propeller of this aircraft and was sadly killed.

June 1979 – Beagle 206 G-BCIS

The pilot and his five passengers departed Biggin Hill for France, but on approach to the French airfield, the nosewheel jammed and aircraft returned to England for an emergency landing on Leavesden's grass runway. Luckily there were no causalities.

Above and below: A minor incident at Leavesden on 31 October 1945, when the port undercarriage leg of USAAF North American AT-6 Texan 44-81719 collapsed. The damage appears to be minimal – even the propeller looks unscathed. This Texan later became D-FDOK in Germany and was a regular visitor to Britain until it was destroyed in a crash in March 1962. (*E. J. Riding*)

Above and below: This is possibly Cessna F150H G-AVUH of Luton Flying Club, after suffering a nosewheel collapse on 13 July 1976. Note that the aircraft's identity has been erased. (*Craig Woods*)

2 December 1979 – Beech Super King Air G-IPRA

Operated by Eagle Aircraft Services, this aircraft was inbound from St Moritz when its passenger fell from the aircraft at 900 feet over Park Street. The aeroplane landed safely with its door swinging open. The passenger was the wife of John Ritblat, the well-known property developer.

14 July 1988 – Cessna 310G G-XITD

This aircraft, owned by ITD Aviation Ltd, landed with its wheels retracted.

9 April 1990 – Cessna 340 N24EC

The starboard undercarriage collapsed on landing, causing the propeller to strike the runway. The pilot and two passengers were unhurt.

8 April 1992 – Robinson R22 Beta G-OPAC

The pilot lost control, the helicopter spun around, and the left rear skid struck the ground heavily, causing extensive damage. The pilot was uninjured.

Fire practice on the wreck of DH 104 Dove OE-FAC that crashed at Leavesden on 16 December 1957. (*Ian Honeywood*)

CHAPTER EIGHT

THE END

Rolls-Royce Closes

As a result of cuts in defence spending and the deteriorating position of the world's airlines and airframe manufacturers in the early 1990s, Rolls-Royce was receiving fewer orders for engines and spares in both the civil and military markets. The unfavourable exchange rate between the dollar and the pound and the relatively high UK inflation rate favoured the company's competitors and put even greater emphasis on the need to eliminate all unnecessary duplication of tasks and other non-value activity across the company. The small engine division was particularly hard hit, with no confirmed orders for Gem or Gnome engines in 1991 and 1992. The support contracts for these engines were also substantially reduced and delays continued to occur on the RTM322 programme. Despite investment in the RTM322 and MTR390, there was no realistic prospect of business recovering to the 1980s levels and drastic action had to be taken to address the situation. This came in the form of an announcement on 8 May 1991 that Rolls-Royce would close its Leavesden facility by the end of 1992. The work carried out there was transferred to other sites. Along with the planned closure of British Aerospace at Hatfield at the same time, and the earlier demise of Handley Page at Radlett in 1970, Hertfordshire lost a unique, highly skilled workforce second to none in aviation history.

While Rolls-Royce had moved out completely by June 1993, the airfield remained open but was unlicensed from 1 November 1993; radar facilities were withdrawn at the same time. The last recorded movement was at 5.36 p.m. on 31 March 1994, when Piper PA28 Archer G-BLFI, belonging to Leavesden Flight Centre, took off for its new home at Cranfield, Bedfordshire. However, this wasn't quite the last flight, as Capital Radio's *Flying Eye* did a farewell touch-and-go sometime after the departure of the Piper.

The following poem, penned by an anonymous hand, was found attached to a notice board at Rolls-Royce and eloquently laments the passing of the factory:

The Leavesden plant is closing
It's all been carefully planned
They say there is no option
They're sure we'll understand

They blame it on defence cuts
And so we have heard tell
On corporate rationalization
(They can flog the site as well!)

Where Halifaxes once were built
At Leavesden Number One
The buildings will be silent
Their useful life now done

While just across the airfield
At Leavesden Number Two
They'll be breaking up the runway
Where once Mosquitoes flew

But the engines that were built here
Like Goblin, Ghost and Gem
The Gipsy, Gnome and Gyron
We'll long remember them

The Heritage Collection
Alas will have to go
They're only bits of hardware
Why all these cries of woe?

They may be bits of hardware
But to an engineer
They mean the 'Leavesden Spirit'
That we created here

And when we've all departed
And development begins
We hope we'll be remembered
In spite of all our sins

When the Cherry Orchard's vanished
And with it the canteen
Perhaps they'll build a theme park
Where the factory had been

With part of it devoted to the
Story of the site
And the part we played at Leavesden
In the history of flight.

The No. 2 Factory laboratory entrance, looking from Hill Farm Avenue in 1992. (*Ian Honeywood*)

Leavesden's main gate viewed from Langley Lane in 1992 (*Ian Honeywood*)

Leavesden Airport's Ashfields entrance in 1992. (*Ian Honeywood*)

The old No. 1 Factory test beds in 1992. (*Ian Honeywood*)

The No. 1 Factory surgery in the old control tower and the fire station in 1992. (*Ian Honeywood*)

The 'new' control tower, No. 1 Factory, and the executive entrance in 1992. (*Ian Honeywood*)

The Rolls-Royce office block at No. 1 Factory, looking west in 1992. (*Ian Honeywood*)

The old Mosquito flight test shed, (No. 1 Flight Shed) looking south-east in 1992. (*Ian Honeywood*)

Above and opposite: Three views of Leavesden's No. 1 Factory, empty of people but not equipment. (*Ian Honeywood*)

The front and end view of the No. 2 Factory Flight Shed in 1992. (*Ian Honeywood*)

The visual control room of the 'new' control tower in May 1993. (*Craig Woods*)

Inside the 'new' control tower with the No. 2 Flight Shed in the distance, in 1992. (*Ian Honeywood*)

A board lists the various businesses on the Leavesden airfield site at the time of closure. (*Ian Honeywood*)

This skeleton staff, here seated in deckchairs in June 1993, locked up the Rolls-Royce premises. They are, from left to right: Jim Lamond, Simon Reed, Peter Banton, Craig Woods, Dave Wilkins, Colin Measures and Ray Hunter. (*Craig Woods*)

Craig Woods, the former purchasing manager at Rolls-Royce Leavesden, is sitting in the control tower (right) on 31 March 1994 – the day Leavesden was finally closed to flying. (*Craig Woods*)

Date 31 MARCH 94					Type of Movement Page 1						
Co. or Owner	Flight Number	Regis. Letters	Type of Aircraft	Flight Rules	* To / From	* A.T.D. / A.T.A.	Runway From	S.T.D. ATA		+ A	CN
	RMNON	G BGRE	BE10	P2	EGKB	0614					
		G BNPN	PA28	T	EGTR	1004	EGPN	10.30			
		G 8RXO	PA5E	PR	EGTR	1000					
		G BJNZ	PA2T	PR	EGTC	1176					
		G BNPN	PA2F	T	EGTR	11.47					
		G BNPO	PA2F	PR	EGTC	1400	EGTC	12 45			
		G AZDK	BE57	PR	EGMD	13.79					
		G DCEA	PA5E	PR	EGTB	15 46					
		G BGUN	PA38	R	EGTC	16 27					
		G BGGL	PA78	PR	EGTC	16 27					
		G BLFI	PA2F	RL	EGTC	1736	EGTC	1720			

The final entry in the official Civil Aviation Authority log (CA Form 771) records PA 28 Archer G-BLFI's flight to Cranfield (EGTC) on 31 March 1994.

The main gates were locked in May 1994. (*Craig Woods*)

Above and below: Xs painted on the thresholds of the runways tell aviators that Leavesden is no longer in use.

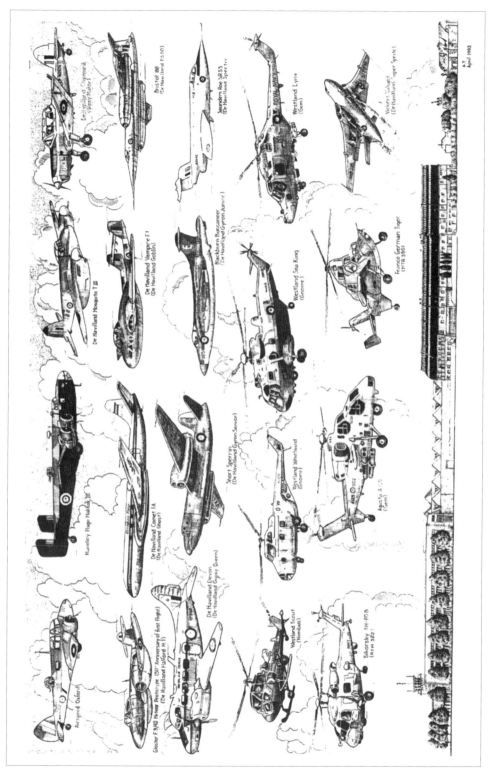

A drawing by designer Anthony 'Bob' Turner charting the engines and aircraft produced by the London Aircraft Production Group, De Havilland Engines, Bristol Siddeley Engines and Rolls-Royce at Leavesden between 1939 and 1994. (*Craig Woods*)

CHAPTER NINE

A NEW BEGINNING

Film Studios

Following the announcement that Roll-Royce was closing its Leavesden operation, Hertfordshire County Council, Three Rivers District Council and Watford Borough Council jointly prepared a planning brief for the site in September 1993. This recommended that it be used for film production, approximately 300 houses, and a major office development, together with a new spine road to provide access to the site and a link between the A41 and Abbots Langley. In November 1995, the site was purchased from Rolls-Royce by the Millennium Group for a reputed £42.5 million and another company in the group, Leavesden Developments Ltd, became responsible for the management of the project in July 1996. Before this, in 1994, the former No. 1 Factory was taken over as a film studio for major productions including the James Bond, *Star Wars* and *Harry Potter* films. The studios contain approximately 540,000 square ft of flexible space, which includes stages, production offices and support buildings, together with an extensive 80-acre backlot that provides a 180-degree uninterrupted horizon, ideal for exterior sets. At peak production times, between 1,500 to 1,800 workers are employed at the studios.

In November 2010, Warner Bros completed the purchase of the studios and embarked on a major development costing in excess of £100 million. This will comprise 250,000 square feet of dedicated soundstages and the largest backlot in Europe. It will accommodate major film, TV and advertising productions within a secure 200-acre site. A major element of the new development will be a visitor attraction featuring authentic sets, costumes, animatronics, props and effects used in the production of all eight *Harry Potter* movies. Leavesden will become one of the largest studio production facilities in Europe and Warner Bros will be the only Hollywood film studio with a permanent base in the UK since the 1940s. The development is due for completion in the spring of 2012.

Films produced at Leavesden Studios so far are:

- *Goldeneye* (1994)
- *Mortal Kombat: Annihilation* (1996)
- *Star Wars Episode I: The Phantom Menace* (1997)
- *An Ideal Husband* (1998)
- *Sleepy Hollow* (1999)
- All eight *Harry Potter* films (2001–10)

- *Batman: The Dark Knight* (2007)
- *Sherlock Holmes* (2009)

MEPC, a company specialising in the development of business units, acquired a major part of the site in September 1999 and set about creating a high-quality business park in an extensive parkland setting incorporating the film studios, known as Leavesden Park. The spine road opened on 30 September 1999. A BT headquarters building has been constructed and around 300 new houses built. The names of the roads on the residential development reflect the former use of the site and include Halifax Close, Sunderland Grove, Royce Grove, Whittle Close and Merlin Way.

Surviving Buildings

A significant number of the buildings from the Second World War and post-war period survive. No. 1 Factory, where Halifax bombers were assembled during the war, is now occupied by Leavesden Film Studios and accommodates eight sound stages, the adjacent engine-test building containing the ninth one. The former DH administration block dating from 1954 is still used for the same purpose and also houses a canteen, dressing rooms and other facilities. The control tower is still in place but not currently used. No. 1 Flight Shed, at the extreme western end of the runway, is currently used for storage and has also featured as an additional sound stage. The Sports and Social Club is used for film-related activities. Approximately half of the concrete runway to the south-west of the main studio building remains, although film sets have been built on parts of it. The No. 2 Factory together with its flight shed and associated buildings have been demolished to make way for new office blocks. These surviving buildings act as a visual reminder of the important work carried out at Leavesden Aerodrome during its fifty-four-year life.

Above and overleaf: Ground views of Leavesden Studios in 2011.

Above and below: Two views of the studios in March 2011 show the new buildings under construction for Warner Bros. *(Pete Stevens)*

An aerial shot of Leavesden Studios taken in July 2006 showing sets for the *Harry Potter* films. (*Pete Stevens*)

Military equipment used in the James Bond film *Goldeneye* made at Leavesden Studios in 1994. (*Craig Woods*)

An aerial shot of the set for the Bond film *Goldeneye*, which was made at Leavesden in 1994. (*Pete Stevens*)

An aerial view of the Leavesden Studios backlot in April 2008, looking west. (*Pete Stevens*)

An aerial view of Leavesden in April 2008. (*Pete Stevens*)

An aerial view of *Harry Potter* sets in March 2010. (*Pete Stevens*)

Another view of the film sets in March 2010. (*Pete Stevens*)

BIBLIOGRAPHY

Books and Supplements

As We Were: Air Cadet Gliding Schools from 1939 to 1985 (HQ Air Cadets, 1986).

Beard, Tony, *By Tube beyond Edgware* (2001).

Cruddas, Colin, *Those Fabulous Flying Years: Joy-Riding and Flying Circuses between the Wars* (2003).

Curtis, Lettice, *The Forgotten Pilots: A Story of the Air Transport Auxiliary 1939–45* (1985).

Delve, Ken, *The Military Airfields of Britain: Northern Home Counties* (2007).

Halley, James J., *RAF Aircraft* series (Air-Britain Historians).

Hastie, Scott, *Abbots Langley: A Hertfordshire Village* (1993).

Merton-Jones, A. C., *British Independent Airlines 1946 to 1976* (1976).

Nunn, Bob, *The Book of Watford: A Portrait of Our Town* (2nd ed., 2003).

Observer's Tale: The Story of Group 17 of the ROC (1950).

Sharp, C. Martin, *DH: A History of de Havilland* (1982).

Sharp, C. Martin, and Michael J. F. Bowyer, *Mosquito* (1967).

Stokes, Peter, *From Gipsy to Gem with Diversions 1926–1986* (Rolls-Royce Heritage Trust, 1987).

Thirsk, Ian, *De Havilland Mosquito: An Illustrated History, Volume 2* (2006).

Watford at War (supplement to *Watford Observer*, May 1995).

Newspapers and Magazines

The Aeroplane
Aeroplane Monthly
Flight International
Hull Daily Mail
Watford Observer
West Herts Post & Watford Newsletter

ACKNOWLEDGEMENTS

The authors gratefully acknowledge the valuable assistance given by the following people and organisations:

Air-Britain; Airfield Research Group; John Ball; John Bellam; Companies House; Dereck Couzens, Handley Page Association; Michael Dawes; de Havilland Aircraft Heritage Centre; Trevor Friend, BAE Systems; Oliver Greetham and Dominic Wong, Leavesden Studios; Hertfordshire Libraries and Local Studies; Ian Honeywood; Mike Hooks; Philip Jarrett; Jill and Bruce McLeod; Colin Morris; Arthur Ord-Hume; Rory McEvoy; Ordnance Survey; Mike Packham; Sebastian Pooley, Pooley's Flight Guides; RAF Museum; Harry Siepmann, CAA Aerodrome Standards Dept; Peter Stokes; Jeffrey W. Thomas; Craig Woods.

RAF Tempsford
Churchill's Most Secret Airfield

Bernard O'Connor

Secret operations, intrigue and suspense... An important chapter
in Bedfordshire's local history, this is the intriguing story of an
airfield with significant international importance.

978-1-4456-0071-0
256 pages, illustrated

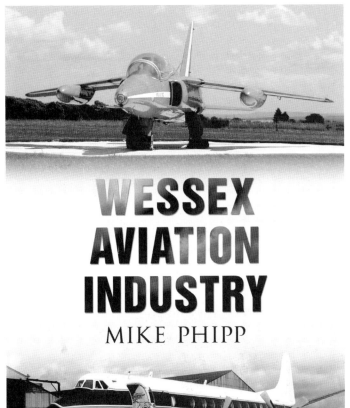

Wessex Aviation Industry

Mike Phipp

From flimsy biplanes and flying boats to Second World War
fighters, jet airliners and rocket fighters – not to mention
hovercrafts and UAVs – this is the definitive guide to its subject,
and a valuable reference work in the history of aviation.

978-1-4456-0046-8
320 pages, fully illustrated

'I prepared my sights and set my gun button to "fire". The two specks
were aircraft. Me 109s. I prepared for action... I was ready for a fight.'
CEDRIC STONE, *Spitfire Pilot*

Spitfire Voices

Life as a Spitfire Pilot in the Words of the Veterans

DILIP SARKAR

Spitfire Voices
Life as a Spitfire Pilot in the Words of the Veterans
Dilip Sarkar

Moving stories of those who made the ultimate sacrifice, as
told through personal letters, diaries, contemporary documents
and the memories of the pilots' families and comrades.

978-1-4456-0042-0
320 pages, illustrated throughout